The
Quest
for
Holiness

DAVID C. LONG

FROM

DEADLY

SIN

The
Quest
for
Holiness

DAVID C. LONG

TO

DIVINE

VIRTUE

Unless otherwise noted, Scripture quotations are taken from the Holy Bible, New Living Translation, copyright 1996, 2004. Used by permission of Tyndale House Publishers, Inc., Wheaton, Illinois 60189. All rights reserved.

Scripture quotations marked NRSV are from New Revised Standard Version Bible, copyright © 1989 National Council of the Churches of Christ in the United States of America. Used by permission. All rights reserved.

Scripture quotations marked KJV are taken from the Holy Bible, King James Version, Cambridge, 1796.

Printed in the United States of America

Cover design by Strange Last Name
Page design by PerfecType, Nashville, Tennessee

Long, David C. (David Clifton), 1951-
   The quest for holiness : from deadly sin to divine virtue / David C. Long. – Frankin, Tennessee : Seedbed Publishing, ©2016.

   120 pages ; 21 cm. + 1 videodisc – (Quest for holiness)

   Includes bibliographical references (pages 111-120)
   ISBN 9781628243796 (paperback : alk. paper)
   ISBN 9781628243833 (DVD)
   ISBN 9781628243987 (mobipocket ebk.)
   ISBN 9781628243994 (epub ebk.)
   ISBN 9781628244007 (updf ebk.)

   1. Holiness--Christianity. 2. Spiritual formation. 3. Christian life-- Methodist authors. I. Title. II. From deadly sin to divine virtue.

BT767 .L664 2016   248.4   2016960531

SEEDBED PUBLISHING
Franklin, Tennessee
Seedbed.com

Contents

The
Quest
for
Holiness

DAVID C. LONG

1

The Heart of Spiritual Formation

Each day of our lives offers many opportunities to either grow in faith, hope, and love, or to allow the deformations of the fall to spread in our spiritual hearts and our relationships with others.

—Virginia Todd Holeman and
Stephen L. Martyn

Our biblical story as human beings begins with the account of creation. God, who existed before all of his creation, spoke, and light came into the darkness. He spoke again, and the heavens and the earth were formed, followed by the land, plants, and animals. Then, as a completion of this work on the sixth day, he formed Adam "from the dust . . . [and] breathed the breath of life" into him. Adam "became a living person" (Gen. 2:7).

We know that God is not a Creator who acts aimlessly or without meaning. He created with a purpose. The Genesis account begins the revelation that the creation of humankind was different from the rest of creation. Adam was formed by God's own hand and the breath of life was

3

breathed into him. God's own breath brought Adam to life as the pinnacle of creation. We can sense something special happening, a hint that a special relationship was formed between God and Adam. But a deeper and more amazing revelation awaits us as we read further into the Genesis story. God said, "Let us make human beings in our image, to be like us" (Gen. 1:26). Something special indeed! With Eve as Adam's complement, these first human beings enjoyed a unique relationship with God. Unlike the rest of creation, they possessed the image of God, a truth that is foundational to our study of spiritual formation as followers of Jesus. Thomas Merton observed "Adam, then, was meant from the very first to live and breathe in unison with God, for just as the soul was the life of Adam's body, so the Spirit of God swelling in Adam was to be the life of his soul."[1] Like a rocket launched on a journey to a distant planet, the intended course of human-kind was set from the very beginning.

These revelations about our creation present a beautiful picture of the design for fullness of relationship between us and our Creator. The foundational truths underlying this relationship were explored in the first book in this set, *The Quest for Holiness—From Shallow Belief to Mature Believer*. Our great tragedy is that sin destroyed this rela-tionship. Our great hope is that this relationship can be restored. The importance of restoration cannot be over-stated. Indeed, when considered in proper perspective, we come to understand that the very meaning of our lives is inseparable from this relationship. We seek restoration for the joy it brings, the fulfillment of who we are created to be as found in this relationship. As one of the ancient theologians of the church observed, "God's image is the perfected state to which the soul is striving."[2]

So while it might be easy to pass lightly over the story of our creation in the image of God, in reality it is a point of great significance. Here image is not to *look* like in the normal sense of the word, rather it is to *be* like![3] It is to know and have the character of God. A bit of reflection helps us see that the image of God is dynamic. In other words, our lives are to *image* God, just as Jesus in his humanity *imaged* God. Jesus perfectly demonstrated this being in the image of God, not as a passive *looking* like, but as an active *being* like.

God in his sovereignty has ordained that his grace may come into the world through those who bear his image. Thus, our spiritual formation is measured by this restoration of image. "This is the heart of spiritual formation—the intentional, sustained re-patterning of a person's life after the pattern set by God when he created human beings in his image, but made possible only by divine transforming power."[4]

But the children God raised up have rebelled against him (Isaiah 1:2), and both image and relationship have been tarnished beyond our ability to restore. The sin of disobedience, a direct result of lack of trust in God, brought the separation which we call the fall from grace. In *The Quest for Holiness—From Shallow Belief to Mature Believer*, it was observed that Adam and Eve left the garden of Eden with natures very different from those designed by God. Though they were created to live and breathe in unison with God, their focus turned inward, away from God. This is how Martin Luther described sin—*cor incurvatus ad se*, the heart turned in on itself.

Thus, as people who look to Jesus as Savior and Lord, ours is a journey of restoration. Now, every meaningful journey must have a goal, and the goal itself most often determines the value of the journey. So, what is the goal of spiritual formation? The answer is stated in different ways. Some speak of the goal as Christlikeness, others speak of holiness, and some speak of the goal of the journey as the restoration of the image of God.

Terminology aside, the goal is a radical change of heart. A heart turned in upon itself tries to find identity, meaning, value, and purpose in itself. "When we identify our self as separate and apart from God—the essence of the false self—we also identify our self apart from everything else. We orient our self at a distance from others. We position ourselves 'over against' the created order."[5]

Since we were created in the image of God but have lost this image, a journey of radical transformation is to be the life of a follower of Jesus. This is easy to overlook when the church is so strongly focused on evangelism, hearing the good news, repenting, and receiving the gift of eternal life. These steps to our conversion are wonderful events, but they are not the end of our redemption. To fail to participate in the growth that comes after conversion is to leave an enormous gap in one's life. Keith Meyer wrote about this in terms of the sanctification gap:

> It is the missing element of *life change* or transformation that is called for in the Scriptures. It happens in the time between our conversion and our death, and it has been missing for the last

hundred years since the great revivals. Our life on earth becomes more of a waiting room than an adventure or journey with God. . . . Many have given up on a life free of worry, lust, anger, contempt, gossip, and greed. . . . Perfecting or progressing in holiness is not expected in this life, despite the many Scriptures that claim this life is the only perfecting place we can expect.[6]

Let's be perfectly clear: repenting and receiving the gift of eternal life is the *essential* first step in the restoration of our relationship with our Father in heaven. It is the first step, though not the final step. It is the unique first step in which we are forgiven by God's grace through the sacrifice of Jesus Christ and become children of our Father. Yet this is but the beginning, not the end, of God's grace.

God's grace continually draws us closer to him. As our initial salvation (conversion) is a gracious act of God, the working out of this salvation is a continuation of that grace (Philippians 2:12). In other words, as we are saved by the grace of God, we are also sanctified by the grace of God. Our sanctification (being made holy) is, after all, the will of God for us (1 Thessalonians 4:3).[7] Thus, we understand that our transformation from rebellious enemy of God to child of God—and increasingly into the image of God—is a work of grace. The Holy Spirit is at work in the believer's life convicting and teaching through the illumination of Scripture—the Word of the Father. While interceding for us, the Holy Spirit shows us an alternative to a life of sinful disobedience and separation from God's will. We are given a desire to live this life according to God's design, empowered to live life with an ever-increasing trust in God. We participate in our sanctification through the means of grace, which include disciplines such as prayer, study of the Word, fasting, and solitude.

Seeing an alternative to disobedient separation from God means an increasing ability to see and understand our fallen *self*. But this is not merely for the sake of self-awareness. This changed view of *self* enables us to open areas of our lives to the Holy Spirit in prayerful petition for deeper transformation. It is a difficult, lifelong journey. A journey that must be pursued by the disciple of Jesus with the assurance of the love of God. Otherwise, it will almost certainly spiral down into defeat.

The assurance of God's love must be anchored in the understanding that we cannot earn or increase his love. "We cannot earn this love, manipulate things to make God love us more or in any way make ourselves more loveable. Nothing can make this love increase; we are already loved to the full."[8] God does not love us for who we are, what we do, or what we accomplish. *Quite simply—we are loved.* With the knowledge of this love firmly in place, we can avoid slipping into the favor-earning pattern so typical of many relationships. Our relationship with God is refreshingly different from the demands of a performance-based acceptance style of relationship. You, as a believer, as a disciple of Jesus, have victory! You *are* a beloved child of God! Now, seek to be all Jesus saved you to be (Philippians 3:12)!

A heart of wholeness or singleness in focus and devotion was what the Desert Fathers and Desert Mothers sought to bring into their lives. This group of Christian hermits, ascetics, and monks lived in the desert of Egypt around the third century AD. These men and women fled to the desert to avoid the evil influences of society, only to discover the ungodly nature and unholy dispositions that dwell within our own hearts. They learned that God's grace is hindered by our failure to control the passions, thoughts, and attitudes that flow so readily from this sinful nature. Their lives of intense self-denial led to the further development of the couplets known as the seven deadly sins and seven virtues.

Most often referred to only as the seven deadly sins, this concept predates Christianity. An early reference to seven chief sins is found in the *Testament of Reuben*, a part of the *Testament of the Twelve Patriarchs*, dated around 109–106 BC.[9] Their origin as a collection is more commonly connected with the spiritual formation efforts of the Desert Fathers and Desert Mothers in Egypt.

The seven deadly sins received concentrated attention during the fourth century AD. They were preserved for those outside the deserts of Egypt by John Cassian, a monk of European background. Cassian originally developed a list of eight deadly sins that was adapted, combined, and reduced by Pope Gregory I in the sixth century. The eventual result was the list we know today: pride, greed, lust, anger, gluttony, envy, and sloth. These sins are the "normal perils of the soul in the ordinary conditions of life."[10] Thus, each represents a means by which the *fallen self* is kept on the throne of one's life. Each represents a tendency to serve and exalt the self, to the exclusion of loving God and others (Mark 12:30–31).

As believers we must consider carefully, in an informed way, how to respond to these perils. Holeman and Martyn captured the challenge to every follower of Jesus when they wrote:

> Each day of our lives offers many opportunities to either grow in faith, hope, and love, or to allow the deformations of the fall to spread in our spiritual hearts and our relationships with others. Free will gives us an essential choice: we can willfully make a decision to allow sin to progress in our lives through giving in to some form of pride, envy, anger, sloth, avarice, lust, or gluttony, or we can willingly surrender to a directive of the holy to exercise trust in the goodness of God (faith).[11]

Again the call to holiness, to Christlikeness and the image of God, is present. Our response is in proportion to our trust in God, the intentional attitude of the believer that enables a proper response.

The seven deadly sins "identify certain basic evil dispositions that determine one's basic orientation in life; they are 'characterological.' They are also universal.'"[12] This comment brings back to mind the descriptions of the sin nature of Luther (the heart turned inward on itself) and Wesley (unholy tempers and dispositions). The seven deadly sins have been present in humanity since the very first decision to follow human reasoning and human means to find fulfilment, rather than following God's way in trust. They are "not phantoms or jokes, but hard-bitten realities whose dreadful effects can be viewed hour by hour. They call for a comparably hard-nosed, tough response on our part, supported by infinite grace."[13] These sins and predispositions of the fallen self are pervasive and at work in all people, seen not only in the conduct of the individual, but also reflected in and shaping our society:

> Pornography is an outgrowth of lust; substance abuse an outgrowth of gluttony; terrorism an outgrowth of envy; violence an outgrowth of anger; indifference to the pain and suffering of others is the outgrowth of sloth; abuse of power and position of influence, public trust, is the outgrowth of greed. All sorts of things including one of the most pervasive and debilitating social ills of our day—discrimination—are the outgrowth of pride.[14]

If the follower of Jesus has a deeper understanding of these seven deadly sins and the devastating influence they exert, then the believer is better able to identify their presence. This enables the believer to open his or her heart to the power of the Holy Spirit, awakening the desire to be more and more characterized by the seven virtues. Cassian observed, "[M]aladies have never been able to be cured nor remedies provided for the ill unless their origins and causes have first been investigated through careful research."[15] If this is true, and it seems to be, then it demands in-depth scrutiny of the seven deadly sins in an effort to find their cure. Such a cure will move us toward the virtue and deep change. Merton affirmed this as a Cassian teaching:

> In exploring these vices he seeks first of all to know their *nature*, then their *causes*, and finally the *remedies* for them. . . . Too often in our struggle for virtue, we pay no attention to the hidden causes

> of vice: we simply oppose passion as passion, and
> ignore the roots of deordination which makes our
> passion become sinful. The knowledge of self and
> of the remedies for sin was one of the keystones
> of the asceticism of the Desert.[16]

The vices are examined as a means of knowing their cure. Their cure, identified in the seven virtues, is sought as a means to a transformed heart through which we enjoy a deeper, more intimate relationship with God.

Jesus spoke of righteousness as something that exceeds the obedience of the scribes and Pharisees (Matthew 5:20). He expected this character to be realized "by understanding each prohibition in the light of the fundamental vice at its root, by avoiding not only acts of murder or adultery but also anger, hatred and lust (Matt. 5:20–30)."[17] Thus, the core theological truths of spiritual formation find application through the seven deadly sins and seven virtues as a template for self-awareness and a radical change of heart by the empowering grace of God.

Reflection and Application

1. In *The Quest for Holiness—From Shallow Belief to Mature Believer*, much attention was given to Adam and Eve and their disobedience of God's simple command: do not eat from the tree of the knowledge of good and evil. Their lack of trust in the goodness of God was at the heart of their sin. This very first God/humankind relationship was the fertile soil out of which came the Great Commandment in which Jesus tells us to love God with all our heart, soul, mind, and strength, and to love our neighbor as our self.

   a. How is trust in God essential to loving God with all our heart, soul, mind, and strength?

   b. How does trust in God enable a follower of Jesus to love his or her neighbor?

   c. How does God make it possible (not always easy, but possible) for us to trust in his goodness?

2. Thomas Merton wrote, "Adam, then, was meant from the very first to live and breathe in unison with God, for just as the soul was the life of Adam's body, so the Spirit of God swelling in Adam was to be the life of his soul." This view of God's design suggests that the very meaning of life is inseparable from our relationship with God, our Creator and Father. Read Matthew 6:31–33; Philippians 3:17–21; Colossians 3:1–4. Reflect on God's design for our lives in light of these verses.

a. What do you agree with in this suggestion about the meaning of life and why?

b. What do you disagree with and why?

c. Thinking beyond the simple surface answer, what are these verses saying to a follower of Jesus concerning priorities in one's life?

3. A premise throughout this book is that our spiritual formation is enhanced when we have a thorough knowledge of the self. This is not merely for the sake of self-awareness. Rather it is an understanding sought in order that we might open areas of our lives to the transforming work of the Holy Spirit. This premise will be applied with greater particularity in coming chapters, but for now think about this premise broadly.

a. What are some general ways in which self-awareness is important in our lives?

b. How are efforts toward our spiritual formation hindered in areas where we lack knowledge of the self?

c. What are some obstacles in acquiring a knowledge of the self, and what are some practices that would help counter these obstacles?

2

Pride and Humility

What is most essential in the process of dying to ourselves is the conquest of pride and that liberation from one's self, whose name is humility. On the degree of our humility depends the measure in which we shall achieve freedom to participate in God's life.

—BENEDICT J. GROESCHEL
AND KEVIN PERROTTA

In the first garden, Adam and Eve were called to obey a simple command: don't eat the fruit from the tree of the knowledge of good and evil. Their intentional disobedience of this command came from a lack of trust in God—lack of trust that God is totally good and had their very best interest in his heart. Closely associated with this lack of trust was pride, which led them to believe they had within themselves the ability to know and satisfy their deepest needs, innate desires, and longings.

We seek to understand vice so that we may ask the Holy Spirit to increase virtue—from pride to humility. Let us examine more closely the story from the garden of Eden, a story that clearly applies to our lives today. Adam and Eve were placed in an uncomplicated situation, their only relationships being between themselves and God, their Creator. From God's abundant provision for their physical needs (they could eat from any tree in the garden except one) we can be certain God also provided for their spiritual, emotional, and social needs. They had nothing to fear as there was no enmity with other humans. They enjoyed what today we might only expect for small children who live in an idyllic environment where their parents care for and watch over them. In short, Adam and Eve were given the good life. This makes their response even more of a challenge to understand.

I once heard the story of a father who took his young daughter to a basketball game. He wanted her to have fun at the game, but he carefully instructed her not to cross the red line at the edge of the court. Before long the daughter was standing beside the line where, with a defiant look at her father, she placed one foot just across it into the court. It was an act of disobedience, a quest for moral autonomy, that said, "I'm going to be the boss because I know best!"

Isn't that a modern-day version of the actions of Adam and Eve when they stood before the tree God had forbidden them to eat from? Isn't the childish act of the daughter just what Adam and Eve did, saying to God that they knew better than he what was good for them? Isn't it pride that underlies such acts? Haven't we all experienced something similar? Pride causes a person to exalt himself and feed his personal and vain ambitions.

How different the obedience of Jesus in the garden of Gethsemane, where he was called not to an easy obedience, but obedience that required complete surrender of himself. He had lived his life in such a way that his deepest

needs, desires, and longings found answer in his relationship with the Father. This final surrender of Jesus required
absolute trust in the goodness of God in the most difficult
circumstance imaginable. Inseparable from this surrender
was Christ's humility to look only to the Father for the
satisfaction of his needs and the fulfillment of purpose in
his life.

In both of these gardens, Eden and Gethsemane, trust
in God was the pivotal challenge. The outcomes would
either give evidence of trust and humility or distrust associated with sinful pride. In the fallen self, the curse with
which humankind continues to struggle, pride is a key
battle. The fight against pride has often been designated as
the supreme struggle because it is the vice from which all
other vices flow, the most savage and pernicious of them
all.[1] This is true because not only does pride oppose the
virtue of humility, but supplants all other virtue as well.
As Thomas Merton wrote, pride "is opposed not only to
all virtue and all moral good, but it *is directly opposed to
God Himself.*"[2] Pride turned Adam and Eve away from
God and his design for their lives. With a clear, uncomplicated choice presented to them, their direct opposition
to God's command stood in stark contrast to the harmony
intended for the garden.

Oswald Chambers understood the seriousness of the
sin of pride, as well as the subtlety with which it perme-
ates everyday life. He wrote:

> We have to get rid of the idea that we understand
> ourselves. That is always the last bit of pride to
> go. The only One who understands us is God.

The greatest curse in our spiritual life is pride. If we have ever had a glimpse of what we are like in the sight of God, we will never say, "Oh, I'm so unworthy." We will understand that this goes without saying.[3]

Chambers said further, "When people really see themselves as the Lord sees them, it is not the terribly offensive sins of the flesh that shock them, but the awful nature of the pride of their own hearts opposing Jesus Christ."[4] Pride brings spiritual death, and it takes disciplined effort and prayer to recognize the depth of its presence in our lives.

The definition of sin is the heart turned inward on itself, one's self-reference to the exclusion of God and others. It is a compulsion to live life in disregard of the command to love God with all of our heart, soul, mind, and strength, and to love our neighbor as our self. Thus, pride is an excessive assertion of self and in effect an exclusion of others. Augustine believed pride to be the core sin.[5] Of pride, Cassian said, "There is no other vice, then, which so reduces to naught every other virtue and so despoils and impoverishes a human being of all righteousness and holiness as does the evil of pride."[6] Lucifer was the first said to have fallen as a result of his pride. Seeing the splendor of his wisdom and abilities, he believed these to have been acquired by his own providence rather than through the beneficence of his Creator. Lucifer believed he did not need God, that he owed no gratitude or praise to God, and that he was complete and fully sufficient in his own existence. So great was his pride and his reliance on himself that he totally rejected God.[7]

Can we recognize in this the essence of the attitude of Adam and Eve? It was not in full flourish as with Satan, but it grew from the same source. As Satan was to Adam and Eve, so there are many influences in our world which encourage pride. Through their temptation, Satan sought to mold Adam and Eve in his own image.

The distinction between pride and vanity helps us understand the dreadful character of pride. Where vanity seeks to be admired, pride is present when a person sets himself or herself up in the place of God. Spiritual pride is present when our fallen self causes us to elevate ourselves above both God and man "and makes us think (at least implicitly) that we can do without God."[8] Scripture teaches clearly that we cannot serve both God and things of the world, and that includes distorted demands of the fallen self (Matthew 6:24). The implicit question of principal orientation from the garden of Eden asks, "Will you trust God or will you instead trust yourself?" The answer from the garden of Gethsemane is "thy will be done" (Matt. 26:42 KJV).

Pride causes us to believe that our achievements come from personal strength and that we ourselves are the ultimate object of trust. Certainly, self-reliance is appropriate in a proper sense and place, even required for many purposes; but it will not provide a complete answer to our identity, meaning, value, or purpose in life. Pride, which causes a person to believe he or she does not need God, is the very root of the fall. Inherently, pride is a corollary of a lack of trust, faith, and belief in God.

Humility is the virtue that opposes pride. Its source is the wisdom to turn to God to find our true self, our true identity.[9] Where pride asserts independence from God, humility is "the place of entire dependence on God . . . [and] the first duty and the highest virtue of man. It is the root of every virtue."[10] When we, in humility, deeply trust in God, we are freed to love God for the sake of others.

The hermit Charles de Foucauld said that humility "is the crown of all virtue, and is necessary if we are to please God."[11] Merton suggested that the only way one overcomes pride is to have the humility of Jesus in his or her heart. As is true with all the sin/virtue couplets, no void or neutral ground exists between pride and humility. As pride dies, humility increases; as humility increases, pride dies. Thus, to fight against and overcome pride is to embrace and grow in humility. True humility is not so much what we think of ourselves and it is certainly not to belittle ourselves.[12] Rather, it is humility in the image of Jesus, who had the deep strength and profound trust to obey the Father in his (Christ's) desire that the Father be honored and glorified.

This inverse relationship is evident in some of the disciplines suggested by Merton to counter pride. First, he counseled us to be humble toward others, thereby reducing attachment to comforts, privileges, possessions, and desires that cause conflict. Second, surrender not only to God but to one's superiors. This obedience, he said, requires that we die to the world. Third, Merton suggested "we must give up attachment to our own judgment and think of ourselves as foolish and unwise persons. A little attention to our mistakes and faults ought to convince us of this, but we train ourselves not to see our own weakness."[13] The wise disciple of Jesus recognizes the vice (pride), exercises disciplines that promote the virtue (humility), and grows in intimacy with God as a result.

This pattern of discipline does not replace the understanding that transformation from pride to humility is a work of God. It is only by the indwelling Holy Spirit who leads the believer into all truth that believers may recognize the virtue of humility and respond. In his letter to the Colossians, the apostle Paul described the life in which pride is resisted and humility becomes more of a pattern for one's life. How does such a life become the normal life of a believer? At least part of the work of the Holy Spirit that promotes this is the illumination of Scripture. As we follow Jesus through Scripture and through life, we begin to view life from a different perspective, one true and eternal in nature. "For you were buried with Christ when you were baptized. And with him you were raised to new life because you trusted the mighty power of God, who raised Christ from the dead" (Col. 2:12).

Paul instructed the Colossians that because they "have been raised to new life" in Christ they are to "set [their] sights on the realities of heaven" (Col. 3:1). "Set your sights" means not only to be aware of heaven's realities as a future event, but also to be guided in the present by those realities. They are beyond full description but include fullness of life lived in union with God *as his child, his beloved.* This is not just a future promised to a believer, it is a present reality. This is who you *are!* It is a truth that should impact the way life is lived here and now. It is a new paradigm that allows a believer to live by a new set of motivations. An essential characteristic of the new life of which Paul speaks is the ability to live today as people to whom the promises of God have been given. Reliance upon the certainty of this gift is where Adam and Eve failed, as have all who come after them. Paul envisions a life that has been and is being reoriented from a life seeking to find identity, meaning, value, and purpose in the inadequate promises of this world to a life of peace based on the eternal promises of God.

This challenge from Paul always reminds me of a story circulating in the company when I was in army basic training. It was told of a trainee who was nearing the end of basic training and would soon return to his hometown. One day his drill sergeant was giving him an especially rough time, as drill sergeants so naturally and easily do. After a flurry of questions regarding the trainee's masculinity, intelligence, and pedigree, the private, recognizing the reality of his situation, responded, "Drill sergeant, you can call me anything you want today, but in two weeks you're going to have to call me long distance." That future reality had a great impact on the way the trainee lived his life at the moment. In two weeks he would be home!

A silly story perhaps, but it illustrates how we respond in many ways in day-to-day life. We get through a tough week by looking forward to the weekend. We get through most illnesses by knowing that after a time health will return. But how often do we let the profound, eternal realities of heaven impact our daily lives in a deeply transforming way?

It's not just that someday we will find our true home in heaven. We are citizens of heaven now (Philippians 3:20). So as true as it is for a follower of Jesus that heaven will be our home, Paul's admonition is that we realize the present impact of this truth: you and I are citizens of heaven! This is a present reality proclaimed by our sovereign Father. How encouraging and important is this reality, that the Creator of all things is, here and now, our Father, and he loves us unfailingly? Precisely to the degree to which we succeed in living according to this reality and relying on it to tell us who we are, we are freed from the reliance on pride to find our identity, meaning, value, and purpose. So our challenge becomes knowing God loves us and finding our fulfillment in that love, rather than in the false, untrustworthy illusions of pride.

What does it mean to live as a follower of Jesus? Paul told the Colossians they died when Christ died and thus, Christ was their real life (Colossians 3:3). This is a reorientation from fallen life to real life, from fallen self to true self. The true self is completed by the realities of heaven. Questions of identity, meaning, value, and purpose are to be answered according to the relationship found in this newly oriented life.

This reorientation has huge ramifications in every area of our lives, including the battle against pride. If we are living our lives guided by God's eternal promises, how will this diminish our dependence upon pride or the perceived rewards of pride? In a life thus reoriented, who I am need no longer be established and maintained through the delusions of pride, but rather through the promises of God (John 10:10). Pride is an approach to life taken by the fallen self to obtain a perceived satisfaction of deeply felt needs. The answers it brings, though, are temporal and self-referencing rather than eternal. A life lived in orientation to the fallen self is one in which we seek our own satisfaction and long for our own glorification. The means by which this is achieved are inevitably maintained at great cost to others. Paul reminded the Colossians that the new life, our real life, ends in glory, but the glory is that of Jesus, shared with the faithful when he returns (Colossians 3:4).

Paul also spoke of this reorientation as a new nature created within the believer by Christ (the work of the Holy Spirit). The new nature is that of a heart oriented toward God, and freed by trust in God's goodness to be obedient and to become more like Jesus (Colossians 3:10). This heart is created in the image of God. It is neither perfect in its actions nor incapable of sin; but it is a heart oriented toward heaven's eternal reality, and by that reality it finds motivation here and now. This new nature allows Paul to tell the Philippians that for him, living is Christ.

Though the words sound simple, it is a profound understanding that true life is life in Christ. Even death does not defeat this, but completes it. From prison, facing every day the worst the world could do to him, the possibility of his execution, Paul wrote, "dying is even better" (Phil. 1:21). He was saying to us that the ultimate outcome of life is neither living nor dying, but rather our eternal relationship with God. This relationship was Paul's reality, his bottom line. As we are able to live more and more in this reality, we experience greater victory, greater fullness, and greater peace.

The revelation of a new life is a transforming act of God's grace. This act not only imparts knowledge of God, it bears the fruit of deeper fellowship with him.

Truth encountered results in the "overcoming of human opposition, alienation, and pride, and their replacement by knowledge, love, and fear of God."[14] As Andrew Murray said,

> It is the revelation of God . . . that will make us humble. The law may break the heart with fear. But it is only grace that works that sweet humility which becomes a joy to the soul as its second nature.[15]

So, how do we apply what we have learned about the fall, the consequences of sin, and the work of the Holy Spirit? The connection between the fall, pride, and humility is readily seen. The fall was essentially a shift of trust from God to self. An improper trust in self opposes the created design of faith and trust in God, and pride is the corollary of (or synonymous with) such self-reference. The lesson from the garden of Eden is that pride does not coexist with faith and trust in God. "Pride renders faith impossible. . . . It is the humility that brings a soul to be nothing before God that also removes every hindrance to faith. Humility makes the soul fear that it would dishonor Him by not trusting Him wholly."[16] True humility brings freedom in God:

> What is most essential in the process of dying to ourselves is the conquest of pride and that liberation from one's self, whose name is humility. On the degree of our humility depends the measure in which we shall achieve freedom to participate in God's life.[17]

Lack of trust in God caused the fall of humankind, the rise of the self focused inwardly and pride that resisted faith and trust in God. By God's grace, through the revelation of a life lived in perfect humility, the Holy Spirit can move the believer toward being Christlike, the restoration of the image of God.

Reflection and Application

1. Think of a time when a person made a statement or acted in a way that you felt was prideful. What do you believe motivated the person to act in that way? How did it affect your relationship with that person? How did it make you feel about the person? Why did it make you feel that way? How did it make you feel about yourself? Reflecting upon these thoughts, how would you define pride?

2. Our understanding of pride and humility is essential to our consideration of the seven deadly sins and seven virtues. Take some time to think about what Scripture says about pride and humility. As Scripture is regarded as the inspired Word of God, you are seeking to discern God's view of pride and humility. From the following verses that reference pride and humility, try to understand what they are, what God says about them, their cause, and their consequences. Record your thoughts carefully for future use.

2 Chronicles 32:24–26	Proverbs 29:23	2 Corinthians 7:4
Job 20:6–8	Isaiah 23:8–9	Colossians 3:12
Proverbs 8:13	Zephaniah 3:11–12	1 Thessalonians 2:19–20
Proverbs 3:5–6	Matthew 18:4	Titus 3:2
Proverbs 11:2	Mark 7:14–23	1 Peter 5:5
Proverbs 16:18	1 Corinthians 15:30–31	1 John 2:15–16

3. Humility is the virtue in opposition to pride. Where pride asserts independence from God, humility is "the place of entire dependence on God . . . [and] the first duty and the highest virtue of the creature and the root of every virtue" (Andrew Murray). The hermit Charles de Foucauld said humility "is the crown of all virtue, and is necessary if we are to please God." Thomas Merton suggested that the only way one overcomes pride is to have the humility of Jesus in his or her heart.

   Reflect on the above statement that humility is "the place of entire dependence on God." What role did trust and humility play in the decision of Adam and Eve in the garden of Eden? What is the relationship of trust (faith) in God to living a life of humility? Why is it so difficult for human beings to live such a life? What does a believer have to know and accept in order to grow in humility?

4. Understanding of self, including one's tendency toward pride, is beneficial as it allows the believer to open up an area of his or her life to the work of the Holy Spirit. Is there an issue with pride and humility that you need to open to the Holy Spirit? If so, compose a prayer for this purpose.

5. Where and how do we see humility in the life of Jesus in addition to the garden of Gethsemane?

3

Anger and Patience

He was asking of me an act of total trust, allowing for no interference or restless striving on my part, no reservations, no exceptions, no areas where I could set conditions or seem to hesitate. He was asking a complete gift of self, nothing held back.

—WALTER J. CISZEK

The Desert Fathers recognized anger among the sins that plagued their monastic communities. They experienced life lived in community and the offenses that seem to inevitably be shared among us. Anger is perhaps the easiest of the seven deadly sins to recognize. The Desert Fathers understood that the passion of anger had to be dealt with if they were to experience the uninhibited grace of God in their lives. They sought to replace anger with patience, the virtue in opposition to anger. When synonyms for patience are examined, they bring in attributes such as forbearance, long-suffering, and humility—attributes that convey the broader scope of patience.

Let's examine anger in light of God's design of humankind. We ask ourselves, What has anger to do with the image of God? Paul gave well-known advice to the Ephesians: "Be angry but do not sin; do not let the sun go down on your anger, and do not make room for the devil" (Eph. 4:26–27 NRSV). This leaves room for an anger that is consistent with the image of God. It is generally known as righteous anger or righteous indignation, the most notable example for such passion being Jesus' cleansing of the temple.

Attributing righteousness to anger requires caution and careful discernment. This passage must be clearly understood and carefully applied. Kenneth Collins wrote:

> We can, after all, be justifiably angry when the difference is great between actual practice and what is deemed just. For the most part, however, justifiable anger concerns not so much the welfare of ourselves but that of *others* as when Jesus cleansed the temple.[1]

We hear in this quotation one attribute of righteous anger: it is most often about the welfare of others. Collins went on to say that examination of Jesus' anger reveals that it was *never* prompted by self-interest.[2] His anger was consistent with his perfect humility and trust in the Father, an anger that could coexist with humility without conflict. "Only the anger of a humble person has the moral force that can be rightly labeled 'righteous indignation.' Only the truly humble who are not seeking their own glory can be angry without sinning."[3] It is just to be angry at evil that also angers God. "Unfortunately our motives for anger are seldom pure and untainted by selfishness."[4] Careful discernment is required to know whether our motive for anger flows from love of God for the sake of others or from the sinful urging of the fallen self.

In spiritual formation, the challenge is not with righteous anger but with sinful anger. Strong warnings against sinful anger appear throughout Scripture: "People with understanding control their anger; a hot temper shows great foolishness" (Prov. 14:29). A further warning says, "Fools vent their anger, but the wise quietly hold it back" (Prov. 29:11). Paul warns that a consequence of giving rein to the sinful nature, the works of the flesh, is evil actions and attitudes, including anger (Galatians 5:20). The advice he gave the Ephesians says there is an anger that is sin (Ephesians 4:31), and the danger in this sin has a well-established history.

It is interesting that in Proverbs the admonition involves failure to control anger, to hold it back. This admonition is directed toward the restraint of the internal passion of anger. Paul calls sinful anger a product of the sinful nature. The question that follows is whether this sinful nature itself can be addressed, transformed in a way to eliminate or at least reduce anger as a response to offenses that occur within community. Is the best possible response to simply train ourselves to restrain the passion of anger, or can the sinful nature from which anger flows be changed? This question will test our premise that as we better understand the fallen self, we are better able to open that area of our lives to the transforming work of the Holy Spirit.

Cassian learned from his association with the Desert Fathers that anger must be dealt with while living in community. "A person may seem patient and humble to himself as long as he has nothing to do with anyone else, but he will soon revert to his former nature should some disturbing event occur."[5] While we can be upset with ourselves, anger most often arises from human interaction, from the real or perceived injustice that results in wounded pride. The identity, meaning, value, and purpose established by the fallen self seems to have been slighted, slandered, or attacked. Humiliation is offensive because it challenges the adequacy of the way we find fulfilment in the matrix we have constructed about ourselves.

> When we find ourselves unable to maintain a satisfactory matrix of identity, meaning, value and purpose in a world that constantly threatens to deconstruct that matrix, our false self is frequently angry at anyone or anything perceived to be thwarting our agenda.[6]

Paul is addressing the sin of anger when he wrote, "Make allowance for each other's faults, and forgive anyone who offends you. Remember, the Lord forgave you, so you must forgive others" (Col. 3:13). In other words, the anger that naturally arises from offense should be replaced with patience. The appropriate response to an offense is forgiveness rather than anger, forgiveness being the proper response of people who are themselves forgiven. True forgiveness and anger cannot coexist. Understanding the forgiveness freely offered to us serves as a motivation for patience.

So, forgiveness is a companion of patience and is inseparable from patience as the virtue that increases as the sin of anger decreases. Among all of the seven deadly sins and seven virtues, anger is the one for which forgiveness plays the most essential role. Anyone who has tried to respond to an offense with forgiveness knows there is a forgiveness that is external, in word only, but far from a true attitude felt in the heart. Jesus modeled true patience and forgiveness on the cross. Remarkably, he prayed for his executioners, "Father, forgive them." Jesus' forgiveness was not merely an exercise of control over an external display of emotion; rather, it was an attitude of his heart, a real desire that those who were crucifying him would be forgiven. Jesus understood a grand reality much different from that perceived by those of the world around him. Does the Holy Spirit have the power to transform our hearts so that we model this character of Jesus?

In this example we confront one of the most challenging aspects of the call to become more like Jesus. Paul's writing speaks of a new life, a new nature, which holds the promise of an ability to forgive that is not merely external tolerance, one that does not leave conflict in the fallen heart. It is forgiveness from a heart that is being transformed by the Holy Spirit, forgiveness that lets "the peace that comes from Christ rule" in our hearts (Col. 3:15).

While only God knows the heart, there are those who seem to have followed the example of Jesus in agonizing circumstances where anger and revenge seem compellingly natural. Corrie ten Boom was a survivor of Ravensbrück, the Nazi concentration camp where her sister Betsie died. Corrie had just completed a message on forgiveness and the love of God when she was approached by a man she recognized as a former guard from that horrid camp. Now he was standing before her asking for forgiveness. We can image what anger would prompt one to say and do in that moment, but Corrie understood that being forgiven required her to forgive. She also knew from helping other victims of Nazi cruelty that those who forgive can move past the bitterness while those who don't forgive cannot. With the help of the Holy Spirit she replied to the guard, "I forgive you, brother! With all my heart!"[7]

Can a heart transformed in this way become the normal life of a believer? One suggestion of this transformation is found in Colossians 3:9–10 in which Paul says the *evil nature* has been "stripped off." "Put on your new nature, and be renewed as you learn to know your Creator and become like him." As the believer grows in Christlikeness, renewal occurs, the passive voice requiring the understanding that this renewal is something done by God in the believer's life. This immediately follows Paul's teaching that worldly rules such as "Don't handle! Don't taste! Don't touch!" (Col. 2:21) are self-help rules, ineffective "in conquering a person's evil desires" (Col. 2:23). There is a role for the effort of the believer, cooperating with the work of the Holy Spirit (James 1:20–21), but true transformation of the heart results primarily and fully only from the work of the indwelling of the Holy Spirit. Recognizing anger as a sin, the believer can open that failing to the deep, transforming work of the Holy Spirit.

These references to new life and new nature hold another suggestion of transformation. In the preceding chapter we learned that it is possible to be guided in this new life by having our sights set on "the realities of heaven" (Col. 3:1). Paul's words suggest an alternative source for the fullness of life, and a new set of motivations that are not of this world. The fullness of life is measured not by the temporal realities (or false promises) of the fallen world, but by the eternal realities of heaven. This is an orientation on our relationship with an unfailingly sufficient Father. Understanding this truth here and now opens to us a new set of motivations by which we may live. They arise as the Holy Spirit illuminates Scripture, pointing toward an alternative life that is more desirable than a life lived under the dominion of sin.

The alternative life triumphs when we can trust that God has already taken care of the offense, so we don't need to yield to the self-referencing demands of anger. When we acknowledge that vengeance belongs to God (Romans 12:19), the peace of Christ can rule in our heart (Colossians 3:15). Thomas à Kempis saw this new life and its new set of motivations as being anchored in the sacrifice of Jesus:

> If you devoutly seek refuge in Jesus' wounds—those priceless signs of our salvation—you will feel great comfort in time of trial and you will learn not to care when men despise you. Instead you will easily bear whatever slander and vilification they cast upon you.[8]

Kempis saw transformation through sights set on something that transcends this world, specifically the wounds of Jesus through which we are redeemed. Implicit in Kempis's observation is the fact that transformation of the heart depends on restoration of trust in God. Such trust is anchored in Jesus' wounds, which offer the ultimate evidence of the faithfulness of God. That trust enables us to look away from efforts to satisfy the false self and look instead toward God and others (Matthew 22:37–40). Can any follower of Jesus trust God for this?

Several times we have observed that lack of trust as an aspect of our fallen nature goes back to the first garden. If pride was the most evident of the sins to associate with the disobedience of Adam and Eve, anger quickly followed. When their sin was discovered, Adam's flawed humanity, the pride of self, was asserted. His pride would not let him accept guilt. Rather, it looked for someone else to bear the blame, permitting him to maintain a false image of himself. His angry defense was, "It was her fault!"

Pride is the vice from which all others flow, and there is a close connection between pride and anger. Likewise, there is a close connection between humility and patience. Pride created a false image of self and anger was used to defend and maintain the false image. Humility is the soil that permits patience toward others to grow.

Proper trust in God is not to be misunderstood as trust that leads to a passive life, shrugging our shoulders while saying "God will provide." Rather, it is a trust that requires the believer, in the words of one spiritual maxim, to "work as if everything depended upon us and pray as if everything depended upon God."

Implicit in the command to put away anger is the promise that anger can in fact be put away. This promise is kept through a work of grace: "He died for everyone so that those who receive his new life will no longer live for themselves. Instead, they will live for Christ, who died and was raised for them" (2 Cor. 5:15). Anger and its desire for revenge will not lead to fullness of life. Jesus' death allows reorientation toward truth in which our fullness is found. Walter Ciszek learned this reorientation within the crucible of suffering.

Arrested in the former Soviet Union, Ciszek, a Catholic priest, was locked away in a Russian prison, the mere thought of which invokes feelings of dread. Through the harshness and the indignities of prison in Russia, regularly imposed by heartless interrogators, he came to learn what the apostle Paul learned and wrote about from prison in Rome. Ciszek learned that there is a reality that supersedes the experience of trials and tribulations. He learned that life is most fully lived when it is guided by the certainty of sovereign promises and by the indwelling power of the Holy Spirit, convincing and reminding the believer of the sufficiency of God.

A new life lived according to the realities of heaven involves surrender of self in exchange for the fulfillment that comes from being loved by God. Ciszek discovered that peace of soul and joy of heart could be found in the midst of the horror of prison "provided they follow upon total commitment and openness to God alone and are not founded on the self's desires."[9] This understanding freed him to pray in a new way with prayers not dictated by his circumstances, prayers actually freed from elements of self-seeking. He wrote that he began to pray for his cruel interrogators, "not so they would see things my way or come to the truth so that my ordeal would end, but because they, too, were children of God and human beings in need of his blessing and his daily grace."[10] His remarkable prayers became aligned with the command to love God for the sake of others. He saw that his interrogators were people created in the image of God.

The intent of the constant interrogations was to demean, demoralize, and destroy Ciszek and the religion he represented. The natural response of the fallen self in such a situation is anger, hatred, thoughts of retaliation, and often feelings of abandonment. It is natural to resent humiliation, an affront to one's dignity and a wounding of pride. Ciszek came to see that in his imprisonment, God was asking him for "an act of total trust," a total gift of self which God then returns as complete. This is no different from what God asked from Adam and Eve in the first garden, and from Jesus in the second garden. Ciszek wrote:

> He was asking of me an act of total trust, allowing for no interference or restless striving on my part, no reservations, no exceptions, no areas where I could set conditions or seem to hesitate. He was asking a complete gift of self, nothing held back. It demanded absolute faith: faith in God's existence, in his providence, in his concern for the minutest detail, in his power to sustain me, and in his love protecting me. It meant losing the last hidden doubt, the ultimate fear that God will not be there to bear you up.[11]

In the face of humiliation, God was asking Ciszek to trust him to be his fulfilment. This is life as modeled by Jesus even before his arrest and crucifixion. Indeed,

Ciszek saw in the ministry of Jesus a response to the failure of trust shown by Adam and Eve, a salvation which restores "the original order and harmony in all creation that had been destroyed by sin. His perfect obedience to the Father's will redeemed man's first and continuing disobedience to that will."[12] Jesus' deference to the will of the Father in the garden of Gethsemane is proclaimed in the words "thy will be done" (Matt. 26:42 kjv). Ciszek wrote of these words, "We often use them as an example of obedience, but they are in fact the most perfect illustration of the virtue of humility."[13] Humility and patience have their foundation in trust. Humiliation is a context in which anger and hatred would be the most natural of human emotions. It is precisely here that the Holy Spirit leads to supernatural forgiveness and humility:

> Learning the full truth of our dependence upon God and our relation to his will is what the virtue of humility is all about. For humility is truth, the full truth, the truth that encompasses our relation to God the Creator and through him to the world he has created and to our fellowmen. And what we call humiliations are the trials by which our more complete grasp of this truth is tested. It is self that is humiliated; *there would be no humiliation if we had learned to put self in its place, to see ourselves in proper perspective before God and other men.* And the stronger the ingredient of self develops in our lives, the more severe must our humiliations be in order to purify us. That was the terrible insight that dawned upon me in the cell at Lubianka as I

prayed, shaken and dejected, after my experience with the interrogator.[14] (emphasis added)

Christian doctrine does not allow for the annihilation of self. It calls for reorientation, transformation of the way God-given self is made whole. This "self in its place," of which Ciszek wrote, has been described by others as being nothing before God, which means being fulfilled by God alone. Andrew Murray pointed to this as a key to victory over the deadly sin of anger:

> If once we learn that to be nothing before God is the glory of man, the spirit of Jesus, the joy of heaven, we will welcome with our whole heart the discipline we may have in serving even those who try to vex us. When our own heart is set upon this, the true sanctification, we will study each word of Jesus on humility with new zest, and no place will be too low.[15]

This is a key thought, and one that requires spiritual maturity to understand and embrace. It is directly opposed to the natural desire we have to exalt ourselves and champion our importance. The more we are able to live in this understanding of being nothing before God, the less there is in us that another can offend; the less the fallen self will seek to defend through anger and revenge. Remember the sin of Lucifer? He saw his own glory and said, "Look at how great I am! Look at what I have done!" He has been defending that false self ever since. Being nothing before God is rejection of self-referenced means of fulfilment. Being created in the image of God means that our identity, meaning, value, and purpose are fulfilled as we learn to live in loving unison with our Creator. Thus, being nothing is being everything according to the design of God represented in his creation of humankind in his image.

This is a difficult process. What help do these observations offer in our everyday struggle? How do we live this new life, this new nature, in victory? How do we work with the Holy Spirit in this transition? It is unlikely to be an instantaneous victory, instead being one that is gradually appropriated as the believer learns more about Jesus, becoming more like him. Steve DeNeff wrote of the fallen nature:

> No single act by God or by man will get rid of this. It will take the two of us working together. Not even a sanctifying moment can cure us from the effects of the venom. We will not suddenly believe in things unseen or value others as much as we ought or become meek and merciful overnight. We do not suddenly like to be last instead of first or to give our hard-earned money to the poor. It is not our nature to trust instead of worry, to turn the other cheek, to rejoice while we are suffering, to give a soft reply to anger, or to value Scripture as much as we value gold. And yet, dare we say we will never learn these things in this life? Must we wait for heaven to become what Jesus was on earth?[16]

I say again, this is a difficult process, and because it is, spiritual formation is to be grounded securely in the assurance of the love of God. That love is the stable ground, the loving embrace to which we can always return, the beacon that helps us find our way in the darkness. It is a celebration of little successes, knowing that God joins in the celebration. It is more about growth in intimacy with God, moving more and more toward God and Christlikeness, and less about completion. Intimacy with God and abiding trust will always flow through the cross and its reminder of the love Jesus expressed there. Gratitude for what Jesus did on the cross is an antidote for anger. Patience in response to anger is possible only when the heart is opened to the work of the Holy Spirit, including his convincing the believer that he or she is always a beloved of God.

Reflection and Application

1. This chapter refers to the "realities of heaven" (Col. 3:1), true life promised to a believer. Prepare a list of several of these truths. How should they influence the way you live your life today? How are they actually influencing you? If these truths are not influencing you as fully as they should, what might help increase the influence of these realities of heaven in your day-to-day life?

2. What does trust mean to you?

3. When trust is placed in God, for what specifically is God being trusted? How can this trust be a remedy to anger and help move a believer from anger to patience? Are there deeper levels of trust in God into which you would like to move? If so, list them specifically, then prayerfully consider what needs to be done to make this happen.

4. Understanding of self, including one's tendency toward anger, is beneficial as it allows the believer to open up an area of his or her life to the work of the Holy Spirit. Is there an issue with anger that you need to open to the Holy Spirit? If so, compose a prayer for this purpose.

5. After having by grace the ability to forgive the guard from Ravensbrück, Corrie ten Boom wrote that she expected to find it easy to forgive. She did not! Instead she found that she had to draw the ability to forgive, to love God for the sake of others, fresh from God every

day. What does this teach about the transformation of a heart from anger to patience?

6. What is the assurance of the love of God saying to you as you consider anger and patience in your life?

4

Lust and Purity

The sin of lust has its root in the belief that God's love is not enough to satisfy our longing for intimacy. We suspect that God is unfairly withholding from us something that we need.

—MICHAEL W. MANGIS

Spring was a time when kings like David, king of Israel, went out to war. One spring, instead of attending to this duty, David sent Joab to fight the Ammonites while David remained in Jerusalem. Late one afternoon as David walked the palace roof gazing over Jerusalem, he noticed a strikingly beautiful woman. Failing at the first point of discipline and resistance, he sent someone to find out who this woman was. The report came back that she was Bathsheba, wife of Uriah the Hittite (2 Samuel 11:1–3). David, desiring her for himself, had her summoned. When she arrived, failing at another point of discipline and resistance, he committed adultery with her.

Although this story is far removed in time and culture from our present, the point remains—there is a lesson to be learned about human nature. David was not deceived, nor did he lack understanding of God's commandments and what he was doing. David had all he required for a full life and the commandment was clear; yet he chose to surrender to lust and its delusion of fulfillment, even at the expense of all others. He was tempted by something appealing and attractive, and decided what it offered was better than what God had to offer. Though tragic enough, the consequences that follow compounded the tragedy. Bathsheba conceived. Rather than suffer the humiliation of being exposed for his sin, David arranged for Bathsheba's husband, Uriah, to be killed in battle. The tragedy of adultery grew into the tragedy of murder (2 Samuel 11:14–17).

God, as we would surely expect, was greatly displeased with what David had done and sent Nathan, the prophet, to confront him (2 Samuel 12:1–13). David's transgression was against both Bathsheba and Uriah, but when he faced his sin, David understood even more deeply that it was against God. Through words filled with anguish he prayed, "Purify me from my sin. For I recognize my rebellion; it haunts me day and night. Against you, and you alone, have I sinned; I have done what is evil in your sight" (Ps. 51:2–4). David knew there was more to this sin than just weakness of the flesh and passing desire. He knew that his very nature was corrupt: "For I was born a sinner—yes, from the moment my mother conceived me" (Ps. 51:5). His understanding of what he had done and who he was brought him to the point of despair and produced his cry to God for mercy. He cried out to God for what only God can do—wash, cleanse, and purify the heart. David's plaintive plea for a new nature and purified desires is heard: "Create in me a clean heart, O God. Renew a loyal spirit within me. Do not banish me from your presence, and don't take your Holy Spirit from me" (Ps. 51:10–11).

Found in 1 John 1:9 is a message of both forgiveness and cleansing. Viewed with these words in mind, David's plea was not only for the first promise of grace contained in that verse—forgiveness—but also for the second promise of grace—cleansing beyond the forgiveness of the particular sin. The passage in 1 John reads, "But if we confess our sins to him, he is faithful and just *to forgive* us our sins *and to cleanse* us from all wickedness" (emphasis added). Other translations speak of cleansing from all unrighteousness. David seemed to understand that something more than just forgiveness of his transgression with Bathsheba was necessary if there existed any hope of restoration of the intimacy with God for which he longed. Indeed, the intimacy he desired with God was blocked. He understood that his heart, his very nature, that part of his being that generated desire and produced action, needed to be cleansed from the nature of lust.

Lust pervades Western culture today and increases in the rest of the world as it is devotedly nurtured. Regarding Western culture in particular, Michael Mangis said, "Lust is difficult to combat in a culture that promotes it in every imaginable way. Lust is most effectively opposed by the signature virtue of purity. Unchastity is countered by fidelity and chastity; immodesty is opposed by modesty."[1]

The dangerous effect of lust is that it "perverts love by turning it inward upon itself."[2] This brings to mind Luther's definition of sin as the heart being turned toward itself.

Lust, once embraced, brings devastating consequences: "Lust takes no thought of consequences; the thrill of a particular moment's challenge or the immediate satisfaction of sexual passion dominate relationship and action."[3] Acted upon, lust takes without regard for God's best for another person. This self-centeredness violates a basic principle found in the Genesis story of Cain and Abel.

When Cain was confronted with his sin against his brother Abel, he asked the Lord defiantly, "Am I my brother's keeper?" This question is answered throughout Scripture with an emphatic "Yes!" Cain's indifference is contrary to the pattern of Jesus' life, which is one of sacrifice. It defies the generosity of God in giving the Son that people might not perish. It defies the pattern of salvation in which people must turn away from their own efforts to save themselves and turn toward God and his free gift of grace. It violates the greatest of the commandments, which teaches that love of God will manifest itself in love of others. Yes, we do have the highest standard of care for others and that standard is only met when we pray for and seek God's very best for them.

Lust is most commonly associated with sexual immorality such as that of King David. In the observations of Dallas Willard, though, we start to see the broader scope of lust. Willard pointed to the discipline of chastity as a means of turning "away from dwelling upon or engaging in the sexual dimension of our relationships to others— even our husbands or wives."[4] As lust manifests itself as misdirected passion, it "is the twisted shape of something good."[5] But let us expand our consideration. We need to understand what lust is at its very core.

Lust has a wide variety of objects. Purity of heart is opposed by any lust—for wealth, prestige, or vengeance. It is found not only in actions but also in imagination. As Oswald Chambers noted, a person can lust for things that are not "sordid and vile."[6] The anonymous author of *The Cloud of Unknowing* brings under the rubric of lust "an inordinate love of giving or receiving flattery" and "a deep-seated need to be liked."[7] In other words, we can lust for approval and applause. The author, a medieval mystic, described with harsh condemnation the life controlled by lust:

> We must also teach ourselves self-control for two reasons: so that we don't lust after the wonderful necessities of life and so that we don't rejoice too much in the absence of unpleasant but soul-nourishing godly sorrow. If we don't learn spiritual discipline in these areas, the power of sensuality will run wild. Like a pig in mud, it will wallow in filthy promiscuity and worldly possessions. At that point, a person's lifestyle is so beastly and carnal that they cease to be human or in any way spiritual.[8]

Seeking to understand covetousness, a synonym for lust, Richard Foster observed that the "sin of covetousness is the inner lust to have."[9] We would agree, I believe, that nothing is wrong per se with having things, but when the desire for things becomes inordinate, compelling, and undisciplined, sin is lurking (1 John 2:15–17). Indeed, this defines covetousness and lust, the inordinate or overmastering desire for things rather than God. This "rather than" is a key phrase, identifying a competition with God for the allegiance of our life. When this point is reached, the worship of things, we have submitted to a form of idolatry "because it puts the object of desire in the place of God."[10] Remember, David understood that his surrender to lust devastated his loyalty to God.

Foster spoke of fasting as a means of grace that reveals those things that may control a person.[11] Through fasting, he wrote, the lust for good feelings was revealed to him: "It is certainly not a bad thing to feel good, but we must be able to bring that feeling to an easy place where it does not control us."[12] Doing without something, fasting from it, can reveal the depth of our desire for or dependence on it. Ambition and power, not necessarily evil in themselves, can be the objects of lust. "We can be ambitious, but if we have a lust for power, then we have crossed into dangerous territory because our ambition has become excessive or uncontrolled."[13] The objects of lust are more numerous than we might realize but they have in common an influence over us described as excessive, inordinate, or overmastering. We can serve only one master (Matthew 6:24). Left unsatisfied, lust can lead to depression and dejection, and even worse. "A consequence of greater harm is the damage it does to one's relationship with God. Lust means 'I must have it at once.' Spiritual lust causes me to demand an answer from God, instead of seeking God Himself who gives the answer."[14]

It is no surprise that as with pride and anger, lust finds its root in our lack of trust in God. "The sin of lust has its root in the belief that God's love is not enough to satisfy our longing for intimacy. We suspect that God is unfairly withholding from us something that we need."[15] In other words we do not trust that God is sufficient to satisfy our needs. This misdirection reveals the deepest harm of lust: the damage to our relationship with God when inordinate, undisciplined desire drives us to seek satisfaction in things God created rather than in God himself. When this happens the believer seats self on the throne, demanding satisfaction, trusting in things rather than in God. Revisiting Psalm 51 and looking at the history of David's reign as king of Israel provides ample evidence of the devastation from David's lust to his relationship with God and others.

This understanding of lust can be taken back to the first garden and considered in the context of the failure of Adam and Eve. They brought their desires with them as they came to stand before the tree with the forbidden fruit. The food and wisdom they desired were not, in and of themselves, inappropriate. It was only when they put themselves in God's place that problems arose. They decided to act on their own, in disregard of God, in order to obtain what they thought they needed. They should have run when they heard Satan say, "you will be like God" (Gen. 3:5).

The problem was that Adam and Eve sought to satisfy their natural desires in a manner that rejected God and his provision. It was a failure of trust. Instead of trusting God to provide to the extent needed, Adam and Eve sought to satisfy their own desires through self-referenced means. These desires became overmastering lusts when they supplanted God's command and, as a consequence, the relationship with God. Overmastering doesn't simply mean that passion controls the actions of a person, in the life of a believer, it also excludes the trust required for surrender to the lordship of Jesus.

This is not to say that God makes trust easy. Eating the forbidden fruit no doubt seemed to be a compellingly rational course of action to Adam and Eve. It was precisely at this point that the serpent sought to drive the wedge between God and humans, this point of struggle between trust in rational human thought and trust in God. Satan tempted Adam and Eve to make what seemed to be a rational decision even though it was in clear opposition to God's command.[16] Likewise, David concluded that he deserved Bathsheba, following his own desires rather than God's command. Every day we confront situations in which something alluring, attractive, and desirable tempts us as a compelling alternative to God's way of holy living.

For our part, we need to recognize as did the Desert Fathers the presence of lust in our fallen nature and open that part of our life to the transforming work of the Holy Spirit. God's salvation saves us from something, to something. In our justification, it saves us from being lost and separated from God to being his children, joint heirs of eternal life. In our sanctification, our salvation saves us from a life dominated by lust (sin) to one fulfilled by purity (virtue). Sin may satisfy temporal desires, but virtue satisfies our deeply felt longings. In the quest for holiness, the Holy Spirit will lead us away from the deadly sin of lust to the virtue of purity.

We are quite familiar with the struggles that occur on the lust side of this couplet, but we typically fail to consider the meaning of purity. What is this purity to which we are being called and being saved? The psalmist wrote, "Teach me your ways, O LORD, that I may live according to your truth! Grant me purity of heart, so that I may honor you" (Ps. 86:11). The virtue of purity is given a position of prominence in the Beatitudes: "God blesses those whose hearts are pure, for they will see God" (Matt. 5:8). Purity is a tremendous commitment in a world that is so content with impurity. Trust in God is the most steadfast foundation for the virtue of purity because through it we proclaim that we don't need the objects of lust to find peace and contentment. It is the basis for discipline that refuses self-gratification at the cost of others, instead seeking the best for others in recognition of their creation in the image of God. Purity of heart sees God, but not in the image of Jesus waiting passively in heaven with our crown in his hand; rather, as Jesus active and engaged in all the circumstances of our lives.

Our tendency is to be tempted toward the easy path, believing purity to be a laundry list of things we do and don't do. This way of thinking by the Pharisees led Jesus to say, "But I warn you—unless your righteousness is better than the righteousness of the teachers of religious law and the Pharisees, you will never enter the Kingdom of Heaven!" (Matt. 5:20). To talk about a pure heart is to have in mind intentions, desires, and the will. British author George MacDonald pointed to this deeper understanding:

> The salvation of Christ is a salvation from the smallest tendency or leaning to sin. It is deliverance into the pure air of God's ways of thinking and feeling. It is a salvation that makes the heart

pure with the will and the choice of the heart to
be pure.[17]

We can hear in these words from MacDonald the call for
restoration of the image of God in us as disciples of Jesus.
The image of God is purity. It brings to mind the description of spiritual formation from Mel Lawrenz, "This is the
heart of spiritual formation—the intentional, sustained
repatterning of a person's life after the pattern set by God
when he created human beings in his image, but made
possible only by divine transforming power."[18]

John Wesley preached about a will, a heart, which
is completely devoted to God. He used the phrase, "the
single eye," drawn from the gospel of Matthew to describe
this devotion. The phrase is best seen in the King James
Version, "if therefore thine eye be single, thy whole body
shall be full of light" (Matt. 6:22 KJV). Wesley understood
this admonition from Jesus as a call to align our thoughts,
our intentions, and our will with that of God. There is no
middle ground, he concluded, for when we are not aiming
at God, we are seeking happiness in something other than
God, something created by God. But none of these other
things can satisfy an immortal soul, a soul created to find
its completion in its Creator.[19] Jesus continued his admonition, "Seek the Kingdom of God above all else, and live
righteously, and he will give you everything you need"
(Matt. 6:33).

Discipline of the mind may not eliminate Satan's
temptations to think impure thoughts, but discipline and
the grace of God can enable us to refuse to allow those
thoughts to linger and turn to action. And purity of heart
is more than just the avoidance of impure thoughts. It is

the single-minded devotion which comes from trust that God is good, that God withholds no good thing from his beloved children, and which believes true fulfillment comes from our dependence upon God, regardless of how appealing the things of this world may seem. So, we recognize lust as an attribute of the fallen self, and pray that the Holy Spirit will move us from this deadly sin to the virtue of purity. Purity of heart is not just external control. We ask to be transformed by grace, not only led toward a life not dominated by surrender to lust, but a heart not desiring it—a heart which rejoices in the knowledge that it is *imaging* the character of God. This is purity of heart.

Reflection and Application

1. When the Jewish leaders were trying to trap Jesus, a
   teacher of the law asked him which commandment
   of the law of Moses is the most important. Jesus
   answered, "'And you must love the LORD your God
   with all your heart, all your soul, all your mind, and
   all your strength.' The second is equally important:
   'Love your neighbor as yourself'" (Mark 12:30–31).
   He added, "The entire law and all the demands of
   the prophets are based on these two commandments"
   (Matt. 22:40).

   a. How did Jesus describe the importance of these
      two commands?

   b. What significance can we find in the fact that the
      entire law of Moses and all the demands of the
      prophets are based on these two commandments?

2. A synthesis of these two commandments that aids
   in their understanding would be: "'You shall love the
   Lord, your God, with all your heart, soul, mind and
   strength.' Another way to say the same thing is, 'You
   shall love your neighbor as yourself.'"[20]

   a. Reflect on the fact that Jesus says that the command
      to love our neighbor is equated with and essential
      to the command to love God. What does this say
      about the love of God?

b. Does the second command in any way diminish the first? How might the second command become a fulfillment of the first command?

3. Returning to the garden of Eden, how is lust present in the actions of Adam and Eve? What did they need to trust God for in order to avoid submitting to lust? What purity would they have realized had they trusted God?

4. We could state the Great Commandment and the second that is equally important like this: *be fully available to God for the sake of others.* Apply this synthesis of the Great Commandment to some of the illicit desires of lust. How does it help give a true understanding of lust? How does it help us move toward the virtue of purity?

5. What similarities do you see between Adam and Eve in the garden of Eden and David as king of Israel in the palace? Consider God's command, God's provision, the human response, the human heart, and the consequences.

5

Envy and Brotherly Love

The list of sins in the Bible are full of emotional habits that damage us—jealousy, hatred, strife, deceit, gossip, slander, haughtiness, boasting, faithlessness, heartlessness, envy. Most of these hurtful, defensive habits of thought and action began when we were young and uncertain of being loved. These habits serve no purpose for us, as adults who have accepted God's overwhelming love for us.

—Audrey Beslow

In the last days in which Samuel served as the judge over Israel, wars and conflicts had caused the people to become fearful of the nations around them. Those nations were all ruled by kings, and the rumblings of the Israelites grew into a demand that they, too, be given a king to lead them. Despite the lack of trust in God this revealed in the Israelites, the Lord granted their request and instructed Samuel to anoint a king, the man we know as Saul. The story of Saul begins by telling us that he was the most handsome man in Israel, head and shoulders taller than any other. The Lord orchestrated the meeting between Samuel and Saul, identifying Saul as the one he had selected to be anointed. The Lord said to Samuel,

"That's the man I told you about! He will rule my people" (1 Sam. 9:17). When Saul was confronted with this news, he seemed genuinely stunned, objecting that he was from a small tribe and an unimportant family. He asked Samuel, "Why are you talking like this to me?" (v. 21). In response to his hesitance, Saul's anointing as king was confirmed in several ways: God gave to Saul a new heart, signs foretold by Samuel came to be, and most of the people accepted him gladly, shouting "Long live the king!" (1 Sam. 10:24). How would you like to move into a new role with that kind of affirmation?

We learn something more about Saul on the day of his anointing. Some scoundrels, we are told, scorned Saul, rejecting him as king and refusing to bring him gifts. Rather than seek revenge, Saul ignored them. Later, after his first great military victory, some people said, "Where are those men who said, 'Why should Saul rule over us?' Bring them here, and we will kill them!" (1 Sam. 11:12). But again, rather than hunt them down, Saul refused to take revenge. These affirmations of his rule, his leadership in battle, and his humility seem to portend a good and godly reign for Saul.

Saul began his rule at age thirty and was king for forty-two years. Sadly, a reign which started so positively quickly turned sour as Saul began to follow his own ways rather than listen to the voice of the Lord. Pride and self-sufficiency crept into Saul's heart. We glimpse this on the occasion when Samuel, looking for Saul, was told, "Saul went to the town of Carmel to set up a monument to himself" (1 Sam. 15:12). Set up a monument to himself? That seems far removed from the young man who was stunned at the thought of becoming king, but Saul had changed. He was increasingly guided by a heart focused on himself. As a result, instead of his descendants ruling after him, his kingdom came to an end, "for the LORD [had] sought out a man after his own heart" (1 Sam. 13:14). David was the successor who would fulfill that expectation.

Still, Saul's relationship with David began well. When the Spirit of the Lord left Saul, tormenting spirits came and he became depressed and fearful (1 Samuel 16:14). When David played his harp, it eased Saul's suffering. Saul came to love David and gave him more and more responsibility. Whatever Saul asked David to do, David did it successfully. Then one day as the Israelite army was returning from victory they were met by women singing, "Saul has killed his thousands, and David his ten thousands!" (1 Sam. 18:7). The reaction of Saul was immediate,

> This made Saul very angry. "What's this?" he said. "They credit David with ten thousands and me with only thousands. Next they'll be making him their king!" So from that time on Saul kept a jealous eye on David. (1 Sam. 18:8–9)

In the life of Saul we see how he used pride to protect and nourish his fallen self, creating a context in which envy flourished; and we see the extent to which envy can dominate even a very successful and powerful person. Feeling a threat to his identity as king, Saul began to fear David. In terms M. Robert Mulholland used to describe the fallen self, Saul became fearful of others, protective against real and imagined threats, manipulative, and destructive. He abandoned his identity as one in loving union with God, who had made him king, instead anchoring his identity in what he did and the title he held.[1]

So intense was his envy that Saul began to try to kill David. He first sent David on a mission against the Philistines, believing David would fail and be killed. When David succeeded in the mission, Saul began urging others to assassinate him. Finally, Saul took the task into his own hands, throwing his spear at David intending to nail him to the wall. His destructive rage from his envy escalated to the point that Saul tried to kill his own son, Jonathan, because of his friendship with David. On another occasion he had all the priests who had aided David and his men put to death.

Saul's heart became ruinously dominated by envy. He had the opportunity to be a great king for Israel, but that would have required him to embrace brotherly love rather than being consumed by the need to eclipse David. Instead, Saul chose the path of envy, in an attempt to satisfy the demands of his fallen self, and it led him to insanity and utter failure. Indeed, not only did Saul fail but as a direct consequence of his slavery to envy, his family and all those around him were destroyed.

Envy is another of the seven deadly sins identified by the Desert Fathers and defined in the *Merriam-Webster Dictionary* as a "painful or resentful awareness of an advantage enjoyed by another joined with a desire to possess the same advantage." For Saul, that *advantage* was success and the admiration of the people, but he was not content with all that came to him rightly (his thousands). He wanted the success and admiration that was given to David (his ten thousands), and wanted David *not* to have it.

It is easy to imagine the temptation posed by envy among the ascetic monks dwelling in the desert, and we are aware of its presence in Christian community today. Envy is not just a desire to possess but also includes an evil attitude toward another. "Envy, or 'green sickness' as it is called, is wanting what someone else has or wanting them not to have it. It is a capital vice, said Aquinas, because it is rooted in pride and flowers in other vices."[2] Aristotle defined envy as "a certain kind of distress at apparent success on the part of one's peers . . . not that a person may get anything for himself but because of those who have it."[3] In other words, envy wants something positive taken away from another so they won't be perceived as superior, so they won't challenge a cherished self-perception. It is a means adopted by the fallen self of protecting self-image and self-worth.

Author Kenneth Collins related two stories that convey the nature and consequences of envy. The first is told by Oscar Wilde about a holy monk living in the desert. In the story the devil came across a group of demons who were tempting the monk, trying to break his faith by all kinds of contrivances, but the monk remained steadfast in resisting the temptations. Then the devil stepped forward, berated the demons, and whispered in the monk's ear, "Have you heard the news? Your brother has just been made the bishop of Alexandria." With a grimace of envy the monk finally succumbed to temptation.[4] In this fictional story, all kinds of temptation could be resisted by the monk, but envy over his brother's success was his downfall. It is easy to fall into the subtle clutches of envy.

A second story, from the sixteenth century, speaks of Leonardo da Vinci when the master had reached his old age. The rulers of Florence asked the highly revered da Vinci to submit drawings for the decoration of the city's grand hall. At the same time, they asked the young artist Michelangelo, little known at that point in his career, to submit as well. As expected, the rulers were impressed by da Vinci's work, but surprisingly they were astonished by the creativity and imagination of Michelangelo, whose plan was accepted. "And it is reported that when Leonardo learned of the judgment of the city leaders he became sullen and was never really able to recover. His glory, which he greatly cherished, had been eclipsed by another."[5] You can see, I'm sure, the parallel with the story of Saul and David. Da Vinci's self-worth was built on the flawed identity of being *the one* unexcelled in achievement. Envy was an ineffective means of preserving this self-worth constructed by his fallen self. In both stories, the monk and Leonardo da Vinci, we see the subtle temptation of envy and its pervasive presence in the ordinary events of life.

Envy comes in various forms. Its desire for evil to come to another can be seen in a sports fan rooting for the team that beat his team to lose in the next round of the playoffs. It's the satisfaction we may feel whenever something goes wrong for people who appear to have it all together. The word itself comes from the Latin *invidia*, which means "to look maliciously upon." The New Testament uses a phrase that literally means "evil eye" to convey the meaning of envy. Jealousy is closely related to envy and is said to guard what one already has. "Jealousy evokes rivalry where none is warranted and imagines competition where none exists."[6] Malice is another component of envy "that truly wishes ill for others and delights in observing or contributing to others' pain."[7] All sorts of vice lie under the umbrella of envy and the harm that has ensued is incalculable.

As we see clearly in the life of Saul, envy can often turn into hostile action, and thus its close association with anger. One need go no further than humankind's second generation to find envy rather than brotherly love at work within the first family in an ugly and tragic way. "Both Cyprian and Basil describe the primal act of human envy as Cain's murder of Abel; they go so far as to call envy 'the mother of homicide.'"[8] Cain in some way associated his self-justification and sense of self-worth with the offering he gave to the Lord. In other words, Cain found his identity and value in what he did. In this case, that means the offering of the sacrifice. When Abel's offering was accepted but Cain's was rejected, Cain's pride was wounded by Abel's success, although through no fault of Abel. Cain, envious of that success, developed such anger that it led to the murder of Abel (Genesis 4:1–8). Pride, anger, and envy in deadly combination.

The most tragic example of envy is found in the life of Jesus, showing how envy can be the response of evil to something totally good. Matthew wrote in his gospel that Pilate knew that it was because of envy that the chief priests arrested Jesus and handed him over for trial (Matthew 27:18). They were envious of Jesus' success, popularity, and truth, and their envy turned violent. Envy was a means of protecting their position (political and religious), or protecting their fallen self. In this tragedy lies the most extreme of the six forms of social interaction that might be taken by enviers, which include ostracism, gossip and slander, feuding, litigation, the evil eye, and/or homicide.[9]

Implicit in envy of success is the act of comparison, the tendency to measure ourselves against others. This is the lifeblood of envy. Comparison in itself is just gathering information and to that extent cannot and need not be avoided. But if comparison occurs because a person questions his or her own adequacy, then it becomes a real problem. "If we are always making comparisons we are going to come out with the short end of the stick."[10] Collins wrote in agreement,

> If, however, we constantly compare ourselves to others, and if we continually define our sense of self-worth in terms of how our neighbors are doing, we are programmed for failure and disappointment and in the end unhappiness. Put another way, the spirit of envy creates an illusory world in our hearts, a world that can never be, indeed should never be, a world in which the self, not God, is at the center of things.[11]

Envy can even attach itself to love given to another. Many are the stories in which love given to one provokes envy in another. Sibling rivalry over the love of parents or among friends for the companionship and esteem of another illustrate this form of envy. The envier acts under the misperception of *limited good*. Enviers fear that because love is given to another they will be loved less. The misperception in such situations is that there is a limited amount of good when, in fact, there is *unlimited good.* This, of course, requires that God be known as the sufficient source of the love and acceptance we all by nature need.

A person's self-perception and the manner in which that image is formed determine, to a large extent, the presence of envy or the virtue of brotherly love. Basically, envy is "dissatisfaction with who God has made me to be,"[12] wanting to be something else, and seeing that something else in another. The idea that dissatisfaction can be turned into satisfaction by envy is a deception. When we seek to build and preserve self-image through envy it is a losing cause. There is no gratification in the sin of envy. One who succumbs to envy enjoys nothing because envy's appetites never cease. Never satisfied, it will only keep on punishing.[13] The success of others will always challenge and unsettle the envious, fallen self with its trust in self rather than in God.

Fortunately, antidotes for envy exist and it comes as no surprise that they involve a reorientation of the heart from insufficient self to all-sufficient God (love of God). "Envy as a sin requires an antidote such as contentment, gratitude, joy or satisfaction."[14] Thus, one antidote is simply a humble and thorough appreciation of the blessings in our lives. The discipline that leads to spiritual maturity (brotherly love) includes an intentional, persistent refocusing on our blessings. This means the intentional discipline of focusing on God's goodness and viewing ourselves in the light of that goodness. A disciplined focus can and will mold our attitudes, causing the virtue of brotherly love to increase. "This is the stuff of spiritual formation;

over time, what we practice forms us."[15] Over time, we find it more and more difficult to be envious of another so long as we walk in a spirit of gratitude, because we are not seeking self-affirmation through comparison. Thus, a spirit of gratitude allows reorientation toward others (love of neighbor).

Another antidote is recognition that things are seldom as they appear. In other words, that which appears enviable may not be so once the real story behind the one who seems to be enjoying such success is understood. "We really know little of the emotional torment and the repeated failures which may lurk behind personal achievement."[16] Imagination and misinformation are fertile soils in which envy grows.

The foundation on which the antidote to envy rests is assurance of and trust in the love and provision of God:

> The list of sins in the Bible are full of emotional habits that damage us—jealousy, hatred, strife, deceit, gossip, slander, haughtiness, boasting, faithlessness, heartlessness, envy. Most of these hurtful, defensive habits of thought and action began when we were young and uncertain of being loved. These habits serve no purpose for us, as adults who have accepted God's overwhelming love for us.[17]

Trust is the reorientation that moves the believer from vice to virtue. As put by Thomas à Kempis, "If heavenly grace and true love find a place in your heart there will be no room for envy or rancor, nor shall self-love have any claim on you."[18] Thus, envy's roots lie in continued

discontent, and in the failure to trust in God's goodness—
as seen in the disobedience of the garden of Eden:

> Faith and envy move in opposite directions. Faith
> believes God will provide what we need; envy is
> sure it will not be enough. Faith focuses on God;
> envy focuses on others. Faith is secure so it can
> bless those who mourn; envy is insecure so it can
> only mourn when others are blessed. Where there
> is envy, faith cannot grow because our eyes are fixed
> upon something besides God. Envious people
> cannot just pray and trust, because they see them-
> selves inside a system that is closed. To the envious,
> there is a limited amount of happiness or success.
> There is only so much to go around. Therefore,
> whatever happiness someone else possesses is had
> at the perceived expense to oneself.[19]

As a believer is transformed, learning to trust more deeply
and truly in God, at last able to say from the depths of
his or her being, "My fulfillment is in God and his love of
me," the cause for envy vanishes.

Reflection and Application

1. Envy is subtle, and we need to be alert. What circumstances in your life call for a greater alertness to the presence of envy? What thought process might help to identify it? What actions or attitudes will help to avoid or overcome it?

2. John the Baptist began his ministry before Jesus, and all the people were coming out to him (Matthew 3:1–5). That changed when Jesus began his ministry. Read John's response to this change of roles in John 3:26–30. What was John's response to the success of Jesus? What attitude in his heart allowed him to respond in this way?

3. Spend some time thinking about this statement: "Since envy always desires something it cannot have, it will never be satisfied." What is an example that would illustrate this?

4. Basically, envy is "dissatisfaction with who God has made me to be."[20] Reflect on this statement, remembering that Adam and Eve missed their opportunity to trust God. Think of a situation that presents a temptation to envy. How can trust in God help deal with envy in this situation? What disciplines will generate this trust? How might this be worked out in the day-to-day challenges of our life? How is this trust in God appropriated and made real in our life?

5. Try to go through the day being aware of how you look at things, what you desire, and why you desire it. Remember the command to *be available to God for the sake of others* (Matthew 22:36–40).

6. Where and how do we see brotherly love in the life of Jesus?

6

Greed and Generosity

With money we have less to pray for. With money, we have less of a sense of dependence upon Him. With money, we are tempted toward the myth of self-sufficiency. And with money, we face the constant stress of aligning our priorities with Kingdom purposes. Oh, this too: With money we are forever fighting pride and losing humility.

—GORDON MACDONALD AND PATRICK JOHNSON

Let's review, as we look at another sin/virtue couplet, the reason for this exploration. We are created in the image of God and now seek to move toward that image, toward God's design of true personhood for us. Part of the journey is understanding the distortions of God's image that exist in us. We need to understand clearly what the sin and the virtue—greed and generosity—are. Not merely for the sake of knowledge, but to recognize the reality of the sin nature. We require this understanding in order to prayerfully open this area of our lives to the deep transforming work of the Holy Spirit. It was emphasized in *The Quest for Holiness—From Shallow Belief to Mature Believer* that our spiritual formation is chiefly the work of the Holy Spirit. We noted, though, that this is a work of

God in which the believer is commanded to participate. Our participation is through prayer, study of the Word of God, and other means of grace, disciplines through which God promises to bless us. For example, when we study the Bible, God's promise is that the Holy Spirit will use that discipline to teach us and move us to deeper levels of spiritual maturity.

Greed has long been recognized as a human failing. The prominence of greed in modern culture was borne out in a recent survey of 123 Americans who were asked to rank the seven deadly sins in order of their severity. Greed was ranked third by the participants, the ranking being a little higher among women than among men.[1] It is defined as "a consuming desire for wealth or affluence, causing one to think of little else."[2] *Consuming* is the key word for society in general and especially for a Christian context in which the lordship of Christ is to be the highest priority. Greed has similarly been defined as an "insatiable lust for material possessions or for power" and a desire to have more of something than is actually needed, "a crass sort of selfishness."[3] The connection of greed with lust and desire turned inward is obvious.

While greed can have power as the object of its desire, it is most commonly associated with wealth. This raises the crucial question of the proper attitude of a believer toward wealth. When Jesus spoke on the topic—and he did so many times—some of his parables seemed negative, warning of the dangers of wealth, while other parables viewed wealth positively, as a gift from God. If we look only at the parables of the rich young man (Matthew 19:16–22) or of the rich fool with the fertile farm (Luke 12:15–21), we might understandably conclude that wealth is something negative. This could lead to the extreme position taken by some, such as monastics who shun wealth in any form through vows of poverty. Such an interpretation as a normative teaching of Jesus would be inconsistent with those passages where Jesus spoke positively about wealth, and Scripture cannot contradict itself.

Therefore, we must take care to pinpoint the object of Jesus' criticism. We find from a full reading of Jesus' statements that rather than expressing a negative attitude toward wealth per se, Jesus criticized the misuse of wealth and warned of that danger.[4] With this clarification, a biblical principle about wealth and possessions can emerge:

> [W]ealth is not inherently evil. Scripture does not condemn riches or possession in and of themselves. In fact, Scripture teaches that God gives us material resources for our good. In the words of Paul, God "richly provides us with everything for our enjoyment."[5]

A critique of wealth should center on how it is used and how it is regarded. The concern is about the attitude of the heart. Regarding the parable of the rich fool, the man's defining quality was his failure to live his life "in the light of the impending eschatological judgment of God."[6] In other words, he failed to live with an awareness of his ultimate accountability to God. Rather than a life lived according to "the realities of heaven" (Col. 3:1), his view of life did not transcend his possessions. As believers are called to live in an attitude of awareness of God, wealth comes with the danger that it can diminish or block that awareness.

A closely related challenge that comes with greed involves idolatry. The consuming desire for wealth, which is the essence of greed, is inseparable from idolatry (Colossians 3:5). "Wherever your treasure is, there the desires of your heart will also be" (Matt. 6:21). In a disoriented heart *things* become precious rather than God. When things become precious it is difficult to part with them and they begin to compete with God. When trust is placed in things, they become idols (1 John 2:15–17). Attitudes toward material possession will vary, depending on whether one places hope in God or in material possessions. Steve DeNeff wrote, "So the way to overcome greed is to shift our hope off of riches and onto God. This is a profound truth; Greed is, at the core, a misappropriation of trust."[7] There is a competition here and the competition is for the trust the believer owes to God.

The roots of the sin nature are buried deeply in the response of Adam and Eve to the question implied in the garden, *Will you trust God?* Believers are called to live in an ever-deepening relationship of trust with God. Wealth, if not properly regarded, will almost certainly reduce that level of trust. "To Jesus, the root of our problem with money was that it displaced our trust in God with a more shallow trust in something else."[8] Trust and faith in God are synonymous with hope in God. They are each grounded in and dependent upon the goodness of God and "the unshakeable belief that God loves you and that he is aware of, involved in, and sovereign over everything that happens to you."[9] Abraham was instructed in a proper attitude toward the blessings of God, including the blessing of wealth, when God said to him, "I will bless you . . . and you will be a blessing to others" (Gen. 12:2). Abraham was blessed by God and with that blessing came the opportunity for Abraham to be a blessing to others and to show the virtue of generosity.

Jesus told his disciples that no servant can serve two masters (Matthew 6:24). We need to understand the importance of allegiance:

> With money we have less to pray for. With money, we have less of a sense of dependence upon Him. With money, we are tempted toward the myth of self-sufficiency. And with money, we face the constant stress of aligning our priorities with Kingdom purposes. Oh, this too: With money we are forever fighting pride and losing humility.[10]

Remember, this is not a condemnation of wealth, but rather guidance regarding its proper place in our lives. Human beings were created to experience life in loving union with God. The fallen self seeks to find its identity in something else. Wealth can easily become that alternative foundation but it is a false one, insufficient and unsatisfactory. This is not about security provided through prudent saving and investment—that is good stewardship and it doesn't minimize the joy God has in blessing his children. Rather, it is about misalignment of the heart that puts its ultimate trust in the accumulation of things, forgetting that only God is the true and eternal source of security and goodness.

The attitude toward wealth or, for that matter, any possession should be one of gratitude, a form of adoration. Simply put, if wealth cannot be held without putting it in a place above God, get rid of it (Matthew 5:29). However, just getting rid of wealth may be of little value if this act does not increase trust in God. It is a matter of the attitude of the heart. "When we prosper, we need guidance and grace more than ever. The apostle Paul understood the necessity of disciplined grace for prosperity."[11] Gratitude is an antidote for greed.

The story of a TV game show host illustrates this. The host told a group of contestants that he was going to give away an HDTV to one of them and a box of candy to others. He began by handing out the boxes of candy. It was not until he handed the box of candy to the seventh person that the recipient of the gift said "Thank you." That happened to be a little girl, and when she said thank you the host also gave her another envelope with enough cash to buy the TV. You see, the game show host was conducting a little test to see who would acknowledge the smaller gift with an expression of gratitude. Do we have the ability to receive with appreciation the gift at hand and not merely be looking for a greater gift?

Generosity's virtue opposes greed. Not guilty or mechanical generosity, or determination to be generous; rather, the truly generous heart, the transformed heart which comes from the work of the Holy Spirit. Generosity is a gift to be sought from God who is the ultimate model of giving. Generosity is part of God's nature and can be seen throughout his creation, love, grace, and salvation. Paul says that the real life, true personhood, is a generous life, one that uses money to do good. If the generous life is the real life, real generosity is that which flows out of a heart aligned with the image of God, a heart of love:

> It is not a sentimental or romantic love, but a love built on compassion and care, a love that is drawn to the broken and fragmented creatures and conditions of our world. This kind of love values human beings as those created in God's image.[12]

So, generosity emanating out of holy love is one of the most evident attributes of the character of God. The ultimate example of God the Father's giving and his love is that he gave his only Son for the salvation of his creation. As this giving is the central act of the Christian faith, likewise Christianity lived out compels giving.[13] As the giving of the Father and the Son was done with sacrifice, the disciple of Jesus may expect sacrifice to be a part of true giving. Giving that is truly generous has little to do with the amount of the gift. The gift of the poor widow's two mites which was exalted by Jesus teaches this (Mark 12:42–44). She gave all she had, which was a deep demonstration of trust. We also find a close connection to the virtue of humility. Whether in washing the disciples' feet or submission to the cross, a profound humility is a part of Jesus' giving of himself. Humility and generosity move our focus from self to God, from self-sufficiency to dependence upon God. The motive for true generosity is not that one is asked or will be appreciated or will receive some immediate reward. In Jesus' example, the motive is love, precisely the love expressed in the command to love God and love neighbor.

Greed and generosity call for proper understanding and acceptance of God's view of money and material possessions, so the lessons learned may be appropriately applied to the prosperity gospel, a phenomenon that has attracted a large number of adherents in recent years all around the world. The prosperity gospel selectively chooses and misuses passages from Scripture. For example, 2 Corinthians 9:10–11 to proclaim that God's design for the believer is that he or she is *entitled* to be wealthy here and now. This particular passage, read properly, says that God will give to the believer *many opportunities to do good*. As the believer responds to these opportunities God will "produce a great harvest of generosity in you" (v. 10). Notice where the focus of God's gift is placed. The same principle present in the blessing of Abraham, *blessed to be a blessing*, is active today. As the believer is enriched by this increase of generosity, he or she will *give* even more. God's enrichment is generosity and the result is more generous giving to the glory of God. However, when the enrichment of generosity is taken out of context and is presented as material gain, it becomes a basis for a prosperity gospel, a distortion of the biblical message.

The Lausanne Committee for World Evangelization held its third international congress in Cape Town, South Africa, in 2010. It drew representatives from the church in nearly two hundred countries and was one of the greatest gatherings of the church in history. The Lausanne Theology Working Group critiqued the prosperity gospel. Although they addressed the theology especially as it exists in Africa, this critique has universal application and offers wisdom regarding greed and generosity.

The working group first defined this theology as the teaching "that believers have a right to the blessings of health and wealth and that they can obtain these blessings through positive confessions of faith and the 'sowing of seeds' through the faithful payments of tithes and offerings."[14] While acknowledging a biblical foundation for some tenets of the prosperity gospel, the Lausanne group expressed grave concern over the practice:

> [I]t is our overall view that the teachings of those who most vigorously promote the "prosperity gospel" are false and gravely distorting of the Bible, that their practice is often unethical and unChrist-like, and that the impact on many churches is pastorally damaging, spiritually unhealthy, and not only offers no lasting hope, but may even deflect people from the message and means of eternal salvation. In such dimensions, it can be soberly described as a false gospel.[15]

Of course, the prosperity gospel is not without its defenders. Writing from an African perspective, where this theology is thriving, Professor Lovemore Togarasei cited positive contributions of the prosperity gospel, especially in regions stricken by extreme poverty. He saw this contribution in the encouragement of entrepreneurship, employment creation, generous giving, and a holistic approach to life that "discourages consumption of beer, cigarettes, adultery and all other practices that many African men in particular spend money on."[16] These are positive changes.

Togarasei is well qualified to speak of the horror and injustice of poverty, having grown up in its midst. However, each of these reported contributions to the alleviation of poverty attributed to the prosperity gospel has a source in a biblical truth that exists independent from a guarantee of health, wealth, and prosperity in this life. That is, the gospel faithfully lived out can make these same contributions and more to the life of the individual and the community without adding the distorted excesses of the prosperity gospel. The proper motive is trust in the goodness of God. The motive for generous giving comes from obedient reorientation to the image of God, an image of self-giving love to which all believers are called. The true gospel, not a prosperity gospel, is the source that calls the believer to such a life.

The Lausanne group spelled out ten affirmations and criticisms of principles related to the prosperity gospel:

1. Affirmation of the miraculous power of God but rejection of "the notion that God's miraculous power can be treated as automatic."

2. Affirmation of human prospering as a blessing of God but rejection of the notion that "wealth is always a sign of God's blessing, . . . or that poverty or illness or death is always a sign of God's curse, or lack of faith, or human curses."

3. Affirmation of hard work and the use of God-given talents, gifts, and resources but rejection of the teaching that "success in life is entirely due to our own striving, wrestling, negotiation, or cleverness."

4. Recognition that hope is needed in the context of terrible poverty in which governments, NGOs, and even the church have often failed; "[h]owever, we do not believe that Prosperity Teaching provides a helpful or biblical response to poverty of the people among whom it flourishes."

5. Acceptance that some prosperity gospel teachers do seek to base their teaching on the Bible but recognize that much of the use of the Bible is distorted and often obscures or eliminates teaching on the way of salvation, repentance, and saving faith in Jesus.

6. Rejoice over the "phenomenal growth of the numbers of professing Christians" but cautious about confusing numerical growth as proof of the truth of the teaching.

7. Satisfaction that in many churches promoting a prosperity gospel, African primal or traditional religion is being critiqued and even renounced, "[y]et it seems clear that there are many aspects of Prosperity Teaching that have their roots in that soil." They express concern that popular Christianity may just be a "syncretised super-structure on an underlying worldview that has not been radically transformed by the biblical gospel."

8. Acknowledgment that many prosperity gospel teachers testify to a positive impact on their lives but also recognition that "many people have been duped by such teaching into false faith and false

expectations" that can even cause them eventually to give up on God.

9. Acceptance that many who teach the prosperity gospel are connected with evangelical churches but deploring "the clear evidence that many of them have in practice moved away from key and fundamental tenets of evangelical faith, including the authority and priority of the Bible as the Word of God, and the centrality of the Cross of Christ."

10. Discernment "that God sometimes puts leaders into position of significant public fame," while criticizing as deplorable, unethical, and idolatrous the excessive lifestyle and behavior of many prosperity teachers.[17]

We must be careful when we point critically at the prosperity gospel to avoid the impression that it is the unique and isolated misunderstanding of God's generosity. Expectations of comfort, success, health, and wealth for being faithful to Jesus are also entrenched in the American dream and that of many similar cultures. This expectation is not the true gospel, which is apparent from even a minimal knowledge of the life followed by Jesus, who lived without a place to lay his head and died with his robe as his only possession.

> Dietrich Bonhoeffer said, "A king who dies on the Cross must be the king of a rather strange kingdom." A strange kingdom indeed. And the king who was glorified on the Cross advances his kingdom by calling his followers to take up their own crosses.[18]

Let there be no mistake, God enjoys blessing his children, but it is a challenge to receive the blessing with a pure heart. Oswald Chambers captured the attitude toward blessings that is essential to their true fulfillment in our lives, including the blessings of wealth and material possessions:

> If you have become bitter and sour, it is because when God gave you a blessing you hoarded it. Yet if you had poured it out to Him, you would have been the sweetest person on earth. If you are always keeping blessings to yourself and never learning to pour out anything "to the Lord," other people will never have their vision of God expanded through you.[19]

In these words from Chambers is heard an echo of 2 Corinthians chapter 9; through our generosity others will "joyfully express their thanks to God" and give glory to him. Paul concluded the chapter by saying those who are blessed by a generous giver will pray for the giver. Hence, this ability to give is a "gift too wonderful for words!" (2 Cor. 9:12–15).

Reflection and Application

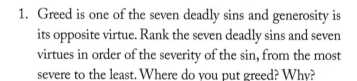

1. Greed is one of the seven deadly sins and generosity is its opposite virtue. Rank the seven deadly sins and seven virtues in order of the severity of the sin, from the most severe to the least. Where do you put greed? Why?

2. Consider the biblical principle that wealth is not inherently evil. Scripture does not condemn riches or possessions in and of themselves. In fact, Scripture teaches that God gives us material resources for our good. In the words of Paul, God "richly gives us all we need for our enjoyment" (1 Tim. 6:17). Based on your experience and what you have read and studied, write out your theology of spiritual formation for greed and generosity. How does your culture view wealth correctly? What about your culture's view of wealth needs to be transformed to bring it more in line with biblical teachings?

3. Place greed within the context of the garden of Eden. How is it present in the decisions of Adam and Eve? How is greed a lack of trust in God? The relationship has been suggested that when a virtue exists a vice diminishes, and vice versa. How is generosity dependent upon trust in God? How does the development of the habit of generosity increase trust in God?

4. Where and how do we see generosity in the life of Jesus?

7

Gluttony and Abstinence

Lust and gluttony share many characteristics, but their main agreement lies in this: they have lost all balance and proportion. They do not see the natural appetites as instincts that have to be balanced by other considerations; instead, they allow them a disproportionate role, and they can end by dominating and controlling the whole personality.

—MAXIE D. DUNNAM
AND KIMBERLY DUNNAM REISMAN

It seems peculiar that gluttony, as commonly understood, would rise to the level of severity to be included as one of the seven deadly sins. While the topic invokes questions of discipline, labeling it not only as sin but putting it alongside deadly sins such as pride, anger, and lust seems, on the surface, to be unjustifiable. It is seldom mentioned in the Bible, although it is implied in verses that refer to feasting, drunkenness, and wild parties. We need critical examination to help us understand why gluttony is viewed so harshly.

Why is gluttony even considered to be a sin? What does understanding gluttony as sin teach us about our relationship with God? We are taught an important truth in the temptation of Jesus, that even the slightest disobedience will disrupt that relationship. This broadens our understanding of the need for forgiveness and transformation to include new areas of our lives which our Father wants to refine, to polish more brightly, so he sees his reflection more clearly. This passion to refine holds true even in those areas that may seem relatively insignificant, like gluttony. A. W. Tozer wrote that seeking God does not narrow our life, but brings it instead to the highest possible fulfillment.[1] The apostle Paul taught us the importance of *pressing on* toward the prize of the high calling. "Spiritual formation in Christ is the process through which disciples or apprentices of Jesus take on the qualities or characteristics of Christ himself, *in every essential dimension of human personality*"[2] (emphasis added). This deeper work of God in our transformation is a natural outcome of our creation in the image of God, a reality in which our Creator tells us that he will be satisfied with *nothing less* than his image in us.

Speaking generally, sin "is the twisted shape of something created good."[3] God has original creativity, evil does not. Evil turns something meant for good to an evil purpose. Gluttony falls within this distortion as a sin that affects people more than is imagined. It started in the garden of Eden when Adam and Eve, to whom had been given all the other fruit in the garden (Genesis 2:16), took more. "Eating from the tree of the knowledge of good and evil was an act of gluttony. Adam and Eve took far more than they needed."[4] Apparently, they did not believe that

God had given them enough nor that he would continue to provide.

We see this scenario again in the nation of Israel during its exodus from Egypt. The Lord brought the Israelites out of Egypt and through the Red Sea, and they found themselves in the wilderness on the way to the Promised Land. Complaints arose in those desolate and desperate times that God should have left them in Egypt. At least there they had meat and bread to eat. Now, they were facing starvation in the desert (Exodus 16:3). Hearing their complaints God provided quail in the evening and manna in the morning with this instruction, "Do not keep any of it until morning" (Exod. 16:19). Some didn't listen. They took more, trying to store manna up for the next day. "But by then it was full of maggots and had a terrible smell" (v. 20). They distrusted the Lord for provision for the future, and the fruit of that distrust was rotten and unsatisfying.

Gluttony may be defined as an excessive desire to consume, normally associated with eating, and one of the points of ascetic discipline for the desert monks as indicated by its inclusion among the seven deadly sins. John Cassian, the monk from Marseilles who recorded the experience of the Desert Fathers, spoke of gluttony as the desire to gormandize (eat greedily or ravenously) and of its contrary virtue of abstinence, achieved through fasting.[5] For those desert monks, victory over gluttony was the first, most fundamental contest against the evil tempers of their fallen nature. Speaking into the ascetic realm of the desert monks, Cassian wrote, "Whoever is unable to check the desire to gormandize will be incapable

of curbing the urges of burning lust."[6] In other words, this
is where the battle for the reorientation of the fallen self
begins. Cassian said further that the battle against evil
must first be fought and won against the desires of the
flesh, hunger being one of the most basic of these desires.
Then the spiritual athlete of Christ is ready for greater
battles. However, he warned that as we win victories in
successive battles, our trials will grow more severe:

> Victory in the contests is never wanting to the
> athlete of Christ as he dwells in the flesh, but the
> stronger he grows through successive triumphs,
> the more demanding the series of struggles
> that awaits him. For once he has subjected and
> conquered his flesh, how many throngs of the
> adversary, how many enemy armies rise up against
> the victorious soldier of Christ, spurred on by his
> triumphs![7]

Cassian taught that the monks considered preoccupation with food more dangerous than wine, with too much
food robbing the mind of "every possibility of integrity and
purity."[8] Centuries later, the fear remained. According to
an unknown monk who authored *The Cloud of Unknowing*:
"If you're preoccupied with lots and lots of food and drink
and only the best will do, you know gluttony."[9] Thus, gluttony is not only excessive consumption but can even be
present in the thoughts or desires for *things* when these
thoughts or desires become a preoccupation.

As gluttony is not limited to eating, we discover that
its scope expands to other forms of self-indulgence. This
highlights a basic premise of this book: our improper

focus on self can be reversed through spiritual formation. "Gluttony is immoderation, and immoderation is not about having body fat; it's about having a gaunt soul."[10] At its root gluttony is addiction to pleasure. As it is indulged over a period of time, pleasure diminishes and greater indulgence is necessary to produce the same level of pleasure. Michael Mangis recognized that while the primary focus is on food and drink, the sin emerges from an overindulgence of any of the body's appetites.[11] It takes on many forms:

> The person who talks too much, the compulsive prattler who invades our quietness and space with voracious and uninterruptible talk, is as much a glutton as the person who can't stop eating. Lust and gluttony share many characteristics, but their main agreement lies in this: they have lost all balance and proportion. They do not see the natural appetites as instincts that have to be balanced by other consideration; instead, they allow them a disproportionate role, and they can end by dominating and controlling the whole personality.[12]

Gluttony began as too much fruit and evolved into an excessive focus on desires with disregard for the manner in which they are satisfied.

The Desert Fathers recognized the severity of the spiritual battle here and its primacy in the overall spiritual struggle of a follower of Jesus. It is a severe battle with self. In today's society, perhaps because of the pervasive but subtle nature of gluttony, a common and easy response is *sin wins.* The message of the Bible, however, speaks to us of deep transformation and the power of God that makes such transformation a present possibility.

Here, once again, we see how understanding our fallen self aids in surrender and prayer. In the face of overbearing appetites, people may forget that they possess a will that they can exercise, one distinct from their desires. Dallas Willard wrote about this in terms of our automatic inclinations, basic tendencies of attitude and action; i.e., the overall orientation of our will. These inclinations influence much of our experience with gluttony, yet they can be so subtle that we often don't notice they are present.[13] Willard wrote about our *impulsive* will, our *reflexive* will, and our *embodied* will. Our impulsive will is motivated by things that are outside of us:

> You see this in a baby. A little baby very quickly begins to be attracted to things, to reach for them, and to move in relationship to them. That's all there really is to will in a baby. If the person does not develop beyond this stage, they will identify themselves with their will, and their will with what they want. They will never subordinate themselves to God and what is good, as a whole person living in God's world. Thus, "I want to" and "It pleases me" are now widely regarded as overriding reasons for doing something, when in fact they should never function by themselves as a reason for action.[14]

Remember the saying, "If it feels good do it"? This is the standard of behavior that crept into our culture decades ago. This impulsive motivation in action here is also behind impulsive buying. A person sees something, wants it, and buys it. Retailers love it. Read the story of Achan in Joshua 7. He essentially said of the items he stole, "I saw them, I wanted them, I took them," God's clear directive to the contrary not withstanding.

Our moral development and spiritual formation require that impulsive will give way to reflexive will. "The reflexive will is oriented toward what is good for the person as a whole, in their communal setting, not merely to what is desired."[15] Whereas the impulsive will causes us to choose what we desire, the reflexive will causes us to choose what is good. But still, danger lurks. What is perceived as "good" can in reality be self-serving and harmful to others. So the question remains, Good by what standard? In the Christian life, God tells us what is good through the Bible and the work of the Holy Spirit, with the ultimate guidance being to love God and neighbor.

Willard identified a third perspective on the will, which he calls the embodied will. "Embodied will is where impulsive will or reflexive will has settled into your body to such an extent that you automatically, without prior deliberation, do what they dictate."[16] If the character of a person has not been transformed by Christ, the natural response will be an inclination toward sin. That is, simply, the heart turned in on itself will put its own needs and agenda first. How is this avoided when Scripture teaches we can do nothing good on our own (Romans 3:12; 7:18). The answer is the deep inner transformation of our spirit by Christ directs our will toward attitudes and actions that glorify God. "My old self has been crucified with Christ. It is no longer I who live, but Christ lives in me. So I live in this earthly body by trusting in the Son of God, who loved me and gave himself for me" (Gal. 2:20). Our appetites are gifts from God and we are invited to train them, or better, to let God train them.

Fasting—one of the means of grace—is the principal remedy for gluttony. This practice may not be total abstinence from food and, in fact, for the Desert Fathers may have involved more of a disciplined and austere dietary practice. In other words, their fast may have been the control of what and how much they ate. The discipline may involve abstinence only from superfluous food and that may be implemented differently from one person to another. Indeed, Richard Foster suggested that through fasting, other attitudes that strive to control a person such as anger, pride, greed, and others, will be revealed.[17] Fasting could be from something other than food as well. The cure for gluttony calls for a fast from some bodily appetite, more as a continuous way of life than a periodic engagement.

Thus, a superficial understanding of gluttony as simply overeating fails to bring to the surface the full character of the vice. As a sin it carries within itself the primal potential for shifting the focus of life from God to things (1 John 2:15–17). Even if present only to a minor degree, this disorientation is something to be resisted. Reflect again on the temptation of Jesus, specifically the urging of the devil that he satisfy personal desire by turning stone into bread. Jesus was led into the desert that he might have this special time to listen to and obey the voice of the Father. There was no problem with bread itself, or even with eating. But if Jesus had eaten during this fast, he would have traded the opportunity to listen and obey for the satisfaction of his hunger; the greater given up for the lesser. Opportunity lost!

Let us put this in the context of our understanding of *justification* and *sanctification*. When looking at the obedience expected of Adam and Eve, we said even the slightest disobedience of the command "was and must be a totally catastrophic sin which would estrange from God not only the immediate offender but also all future descendants and indeed all future humanity."[18] Jesus gave himself on the cross for the forgiveness of disobedience so that the estrangement from God might, by grace, be removed (justification). But God is not content to allow the fallen self to remain untouched in his beloved children. Gluttony is not the image our Creator desires to see in us. Instead, as we trust him, he forms his image in us (sanctification).

You may be reading this and still questioning, What's the big deal? Well, gluttony may be a *really* big deal. It can prevent our spiritual journey from entering into a place where God desires to speak to us, or block us from the studied discipline of hearing that voice because we seek satisfaction in something else. It may just be a missed opportunity to seek God and put him first; in other words, to grow in Christlikeness. In some way, flagrant or subtle, something created for good is used with harmful results, including lack of trust in God. The end result of the practice of abstinence is training in gratitude for the provisions of God, training that is especially beneficial and necessary in cultures where there is an overabundance of food and other things. A further benefit closely connected with gratitude is trust in God for his continued provision. It is not until our attention is taken off of things and put on God that we can offer true gratitude to God.

As with all of the seven deadly sins, the specter of a heart turned in on itself (*cor incurvatus ad se*) is present in gluttony. When the voice motivating from within says *I deserve it! I'm worth it!*, it may be calling for a disregard of the virtue of abstinence. If a disciple of Jesus is thought of as one of living and breathing in unison with God, there is something in the presence of gluttony that strikes a note of discord. It is a vice that simply leads away from a path of discipline and is broad in its attack. The virtue of abstinence says "I can do without anything in excess," and is aided by deep trust in the goodness of God. Perhaps, as I do, you hear the voice of Jesus saying, "Remain in me, and I will remain in you" (John 15:4). The virtue of abstinence is a means to a life of contentment in which the peace of Christ reigns.

So, back to our earlier thought, *Does sin win?* Without the enabling presence of the Holy Spirit, sin does win.

> In direct confrontation between human flesh and human spirit, between what is desired and what is good, sin wins. The futile human struggle with evil proves it. But fellowship with Jesus Christ in the new life from above brings new possibilities into play on the side of the human spirit in carrying out its intentions for good. Sin then loses

as the desires of the flesh are ordered under the goodness and power of God in us.[19]

Awareness and understanding of our sin nature and surrendering to the indwelling power of the Holy Spirit will result in transformation. That is a promise. It may take a long, long time or even a lifetime as this salvation is worked out in our life, but it is a promise. "So I say, let the Holy Spirit guide your lives. Then you won't be doing what your sinful nature craves" (Gal. 5:16). What a good time to rest in the assurance of the love of God, the love of a Father who wants for you his very best!

Reflection and Application

1. Gluttony is excessive desire for more than just food. What are other objects of gluttony in your culture?

2. The Desert Fathers said victory over gluttony was the first and most fundamental victory against the evil tempers (dispositions) of the fallen self. Why might this be true? How is fasting an antidote to gluttony even in the context of its broader meanings? Don't be concerned if there is no clear distinction between gluttony and other vices such as lust or greed. There is much overlap and interaction among them.

3. Gluttony in the form of overeating can bring with it issues of self-esteem, and distorted views of self. Reflect on God's love and the assurance you have of that love. How deep is that assurance? How much does the love of God form your identity? How might you continually live in this truth of God's love? How can this empower/encourage you to give God access to the dark parts of your soul that need transformation?

4. Putting it in terms of gluttony and abstinence and within the context of the garden of Eden, describe how gluttony caused Adam and Eve to miss an opportunity to place their trust in God.

5. The temptation to gluttony is present in the life of every believer. Write a prayer or psalm expressing yourself, perhaps a confession, perhaps a petition, or a commitment to God.

8

Sloth and Perseverance

Sloth is most often evidenced in busyness . . . in frantic running around, trying to be everything to everyone, and then having no time to listen or pray, no time to become the person who is doing these things.

—Eugene Peterson

As we come to the last of the seven deadly sins, let us take this opportunity to review the highlights of this journey of spiritual formation. It begins, appropriately, in the beginning of God's revelation. In the first chapter of the first book of the Bible, God reveals to us that he created humankind in his image. This revelation lays the foundation of our spiritual formation, the call of God to his children to live this image. It calls us to a life of both *doing* and *being*. From this revelation of a pattern in God's creative design we find our identity, value, meaning, and purpose. It bears repeating that "this is the heart of spiritual formation—the intentional, sustained re-patterning of a person's life after the pattern set by God when he created human beings in his image, but made possible only by divine transforming power."[1]

99

The great tragedy of human existence is that our own choices separate us from our Creator by the sin of disobedience, which is directly related to trust in God. This lack of trust is the fallen nature or fallen self that became part of humankind from the sin of Adam and Eve forward, the fallen nature by which all of humankind is cursed. Martin Luther described it in the phrase *cor incurvatus ad se*, the heart turned in upon itself.

The remedy for this fallen nature and the separation from God is not within ourselves. We are totally dependent on God. Thus, we read that we are saved (justified) by the grace of God through faith (Ephesians 2:8). John Wesley's oft-used phrase for this is *sola gratia et fides*, only grace by faith. But when God saves us from something, he always saves us to something. We see this, for example, in the nation of Israel. God freed the Israelites from the slavery of Egypt but his salvation of Israel did not stop there. God led them to the Promised Land and did so in order that they might become the people of God. God saved them from slavery to being his people. Likewise, when the apostle Paul says we are to work out our salvation "with deep reverence and fear" (Phil. 2:12), he is saying that God not only saves us out of our slavery to sin, he is also saving us into being his children. We are saved from something to something.

God saves us out of our lostness and separation from him to an ever-deepening relationship with him. We must understand that God did not save us just so we would someday escape the fires of hell and go to heaven. This deepening of our relationship with him begins here and now! God saves us for this growing, eternal relationship. As it must have something it grows toward, we come to understand this end as Christlikeness, and since Jesus is the "exact imprint" of God's nature (Heb. 1:3 NRSV), this is growth or maturity toward the image of God. The most descriptive term for this image is holiness.

That's pretty intimidating. Our natural response is *I could never do that!* And in that we are right. Just as our conversion (justification) comes by the grace of God, so our being conformed to the image of God (sanctification) comes by that same grace. It is a work of the indwelling Holy Spirit. Terminology aside, the goal of our spiritual formation is a radical change of heart.

We are called to know Jesus as Savior through our justification, and Jesus as Lord of our lives, as his disciples, through our sanctification. This latter is a demanding, lifelong journey, one that must be taken with awareness of the continual, loving embrace of our Father in heaven. We pursue it in the assurance that in success or in failure, God's love for us is constant. We live in the assurance that as the Father loves the Son, so we, too, are beloved. "Nothing is so fundamental to the Christian journey as knowing and feeling that we are loved. Nothing."[2] This is the basis for the whole of what it means to be a Christian. There is no other foundation on which we can build. It is from the experience of God's love that we know the grace of God and live out every other dimension of our Christian faith.

So, let's turn to the seventh of the deadly sins and divine virtues. "Sloth poses as love of peace: yet what certain peace is there beside the Lord?"[3] Sloth is the deadly sin commonly thought of as laziness, but sloth involves much more than just the modern concept of the couch potato.[4] Understanding what sloth really is gives us deeper insight into our human nature. The ancients recognized sloth as deadly because it has the capacity to destroy the Christian's commitment to redeeming engagement with the world, relationships with others, and even one's relationship with God.

Thomas Aquinas defined sloth as "annoyance or sadness about spiritual and inner good."[5] *Complacency* is the contemporary expression that best describes sloth. *Boredom* also captures the meaning of sloth, as when one becomes bored with the pursuit of his or her greatest good. It is boredom with the pursuit of the highest calling in life. We hear the opposite of sloth in Paul's admonitions to run the race, to press on, to be people of discipline. Sloth is abandoning the race, while perseverance is the commitment to continue. A goal of this book is to help us understand that this race is an essential part of living this life in truth.

The modern tendency to equate sloth simply with laziness can obscure the presence of this particular curse of the human nature and the extent of its danger. It's so easy to charge forward with great vigor toward the wrong goal! Busyness and hard work are often assumed to be the opposite of sloth, but they can disguise a dangerous form of sloth, spiritual laziness. In fact, Eugene Peterson said, "Sloth is most often evidenced in busyness . . . in frantic running around, trying to be everything to everyone, and then having no time to listen or pray, no time to become the person who is doing these things."[6] Busyness and hard work can blind us to the more important things that bring us into the presence of God. We remember that Elijah did not find the Lord in the wind or the earthquake or the fire, but in the sound of a low whisper (1 Kings 19:11–12). Busyness and noise can cause this low whisper to be missed. The mandate of the disciple of Jesus is to pay attention to Jesus and to focus the activities of life on deepening one's relationship with Jesus. Busyness that inhibits or, very often, completely prevents the development of this relationship is damaging. Allowing this situation to persist is spiritual sloth.

The classic tension in spiritual sloth is between *being* and *doing*. It is a simple fact that *doing* can deflect attention from *being* and sap the energy *being* requires. This tension is illustrated in the story of the sisters Martha and Mary. With visitors in the home, Martha was busy with preparations to care for these guests. Her sister Mary sat at Jesus' feet as he talked. Replying to Martha's complaint that Mary was just listening and not helping care for their guests, Jesus replied that Martha was anxious and distracted concerning many things (Luke 10:41). He said to her, "There is only one thing worth being concerned about. Mary has discovered it, and it will not be taken away from her" (v. 42). In this instruction to Martha, Jesus was not condemning *doing*. Disciples of Jesus are called to have both a spirituality of being and a spirituality of doing. In this manner being and doing do not reject each other; they are complementary. Jesus did not reject the activity of Martha. He rejected the separation her activities caused between her and himself. He rejected activities that were not anointed by grace and which in effect inhibited the flow of grace.

From the story of these sisters a deeper understanding of sloth emerges. It is not simply laziness that fails to make the bed, do the dishes, or read a good book from time to time. Sloth is inattention to one's relationship with God. "Sloth is the neglect of the greatest commandment: to love the Lord your God with all your heart, soul, mind and strength."[7] The *all* in this command sets the intensity expected to be found in our response. Sloth is also neglect of the second commandment to love our neighbor. It is laziness or apathy with regard to deepening our relationship with God, and hence, our neighbor. It is neglect of sanctification, the very heart of the life calling of a follower of Jesus. Sloth is a response to the call to spiritual formation that says, "I'll take heaven in the next life, but I really don't care about the lordship of Jesus in this life."

The word *sloth* grew out of the earlier use of *sadness* and *acedia* as descriptive of a way of acting and thinking. As Cassian reported from living with the Desert Fathers, the malady known as the "noonday demon" caused the monks to have difficulty in "concentrating on the ascetic and mystical experience."[8] In other words, this affliction of sloth caused the monks to have difficulty applying themselves to the life to which they had committed. Thomas Merton would add to this description difficulty in being pleasant and charitable with others, and impatience.[9] However, the devastation of sloth can be much deeper, even causing a person to lose the sense and assurance that God is working for good in his or her life. Sloth can cause one to come to believe that God's goodness does not exist, or that it "no longer encompasses [our] life."[10] Sloth can cause a person to say, "If God is good, he is not good for me."

The fifteenth-century Russian saint Nil Sorsky saw in sloth the loss of hope that suffering would end. The monk who succumbed to sloth thought God had abandoned him and no longer cared for him. He believed his suffering was outside the care of God and God's divine providence. Thinking that only he was suffering in this way, sloth caused him to be overwhelmed by these thoughts to such an extent that he gave up hope.[11] A glimpse of this despair and hopelessness can be seen in this dialogue of Job:

> I have only a few days left, so leave me alone, that I may have a moment of comfort before I leave—never to return—for the land of darkness and utter gloom. It is a land as dark as midnight, a land of gloom and confusion, where even the light is dark as midnight. (Job 10:20–22)

Remembering Job's desire to present his case to God and be declared innocent, Jeff Vogel's definition of sloth (acedia) seems plausible: "*Acedia* might best be described as distress caused by the evident slowness of God's activity, impatience with having to inhabit the condition of the *viator*, revulsion, even, at having to wait on God"[12]

In Job, in Martha, and in the desert monk, we observe a lack of trust in the grace of God. Indeed, an inadequate embrace of the grace of God is at the core of each of the seven deadly sins. Applied specifically to sloth: "If waiting on God can be said to be the Christian vocation par excellence, *acedia* can be said to constitute the chief temptation to the Christian state of life."[13] This sheds light on the virtue. Virtue calls us to persevere in faith. Perseverance may involve doing, but in waiting on God it will always involve being. This being is the trustful abiding which Jesus taught in John 15. "Remain in me, and I will remain in you. For a branch cannot produce fruit if it is severed from the vine, and you cannot be fruitful unless you remain in me" (v. 4). I like the word "abide" rather than "remain" to translate the Greek verb μένω in this passage. It is continual watchfulness and trusting expectation with a sense of unhurriedness and peace.

The apostle Paul gave instructions that relate to sloth, both in the admonitions in his letters and in his life. Paul's life was one of perseverance through surrender as an apostle and as a missionary, whether traveling, preaching, teaching, or when confined to prison in Rome. Paul described the life of a disciple in athletic terms, urging followers of Jesus to engage in strict training (1 Corinthians 9:24), to press on toward that to which God has called (Philippians 3:14). Such trust and commitment are the opposite of sloth.

If ever there was a circumstance that would seem to justify spiritual sloth, it would be in the arrest and crucifixion of Jesus. Toward the Father he lived a perfect life, surrendered and sinless. Toward humankind he sought only that which was good, and their accusations of him were devastatingly unfounded. Yet, as he experienced the cross, he never abandoned his trust in the Father's sovereignty and goodness. Although he had to experience the forsakenness of the cross as the bearer of sin (Matthew 27:46), he persevered in trust in the Father. Among his last words on the cross were words of deep trust, "Father, I entrust my spirit into your hands" (Luke 23:46).

In our journey toward the image of God, sloth bids us to stop by the wayside. The conclusion that reasonably follows is that the antidote to sloth is immersion in the means of grace, the means by which the follower of Jesus attends to his or her relationship with God. Immersion in the means of grace comes through commitment to prayer, Bible study, Holy Communion, doing good in our community, and active involvement in the ministries of our church, including its mission of taking the gospel to the ends of the earth.

Perseverance through the means of grace is both doing and being. Whereas sloth "must spring from a distaste for the divine good,"[14] the means of grace invite believers to pursue and satisfy the longing for divine good. The oft-heard admonition among Christian writers is that the proper response to sloth is that "one must stand still and fight."[15] Flight into busyness or any other activity taken to ease the tension of waiting on God only strengthens the noonday demon and invites continued attacks. "It is not without reason, then, that the tradition holds that acedia, alone among the vices, must be met and not fled. God alone can end the waiting; human beings can only endure."[16] In the face of all things that seem to indicate or compel the contrary, the believer must persevere in the confidence of (trust in) the love and divine sovereignty of God, a perseverance seen most supremely in the passion of Jesus. The obedience of Jesus, his trust in the Father, and the Father's trustworthiness are inseparable.

Gracious and loving God, I praise you and offer my gratitude for the way you have made me:

By your grace you have brought me from one lost in my rebellion to eternal blessing as one of your beloved children;

Help me surrender more and more to your loving will that I may be all that you saved me to be;

Restore me to Christlikeness, to your own image, that
I might live in loving union with you;

I confess my sin and my need for you to cleanse me
from all unrighteousness and to create in me a
clean heart;

Where there is sloth, help me to see it and to move
toward perseverance in ways that honor you;

Where there is gluttony, teach me the joy of living a
life of abstinence from anything that separates
me from you;

Where there is greed, grant that I may show love of
my neighbor through generosity;

Where there is envy, help me to find such fullness in
your providence that I may be freed for brotherly
love;

Where there is lust, may I be drawn by the thought of
your pristine purity to a true way of living;

Where there is anger, may the example of your patience
with me lead me to show loving patience to those
around me;

Where there is pride, O that sinful pride, break my
heart with the memory of Jesus who had the
humility to endure the cross;

By the power of the indwelling Holy Spirit for your
eternal honor and unbounded glory. Amen.

Reflection and Application

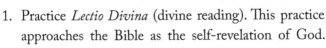

1. Practice *Lectio Divina* (divine reading). This practice approaches the Bible as the self-revelation of God. Here is a description of the practice:

   a. **Reading**. Gently read the passage of Scripture aloud, being mindful of each word and phrase. The goal is not to read large quantities of Scripture, but to engage it reflectively and with an awareness of God's presence. This may mean reading the text multiple times. Eventually identify a word or short phrase that speaks to you in some manner.

   b. **Meditating**. Having read the Scripture, in the second movement allow the Scriptures to "read you." Use the passage or phrase to guide your time of reflection and self-examination. How does the reading apply to you and your circumstances? Invite God to speak and reveal what he desires to impart to you through the text.

   c. **Speaking**. After allowing God and his Scripture to have the first word, it is now time for you to respond. Communicate your thoughts to God with words. This may be gratitude, confession, worry, joy, or any number of emotions that result from engaging the Scripture.

   d. **Contemplating**. When speaking ceases, it is time to rest in God's presence. Use the remainder of the time to be silent and open to what God has to say.

Receive his forgiveness, assurance, or whatever he may have for you.

e. **Ruminating**. As you conclude your time, take the special word or phrase from the reading with you. Throughout the day return to it as a prompt for prayer and as a reminder of God's presence with you.

2. Read Luke 10:38–42. Jesus came to the home of Martha as a traveler. Middle Eastern culture called for the host to extend a welcome and hospitality to him. Martha's activities were surely consistent with the cultural expectations. However, Jesus was more than an ordinary traveler. When Jesus entered, there was a drawing near of the kingdom of heaven. Practice *Lectio Divina* with this passage. What was uppermost on Martha's mind? On Mary's? How are sloth and perseverance illuminated in this passage?

Notes

Chapter 1: The Heart of Spiritual Formation

1. Thomas Merton, *The New Man* (New York: Farrar, Straus and Giroux, 1962), 53.

2. Anders Lund Jacobsen, "Genesis 1–3 as Source for the Anthropology of Origen," *Vigiliae Christianae* 62.3 (2008): 213–32.

3. In *The Quest for Holiness—From Shallow Belief to Mature Believer*, the limitation in this likeness was discussed (p. 8). God is always separate from his creation. We grow in the likeness of God's character, but never share in God's essence. Note carefully that God is and will always be *other* than his creation. We, by grace, may share in the character of God (i.e., love of neighbor), but we never share in the divine essence of God.

4. Mel Lawrenz, *The Dynamics of Spiritual Formation* (Grand Rapids, MI: Baker Books, 2000), 145–46.

5. M. Robert Mulholland Jr., *The Deeper Journey: The Spirituality of Discovering Your True Self* (Downers Grove, IL: IVP Books, 2006), 29.

6. Keith Meyer, "Whole-Life Transformation," in Alan Andrews, ed., *The Kingdom Life: A Practical Theology of Discipleship and Spiritual Formation* (Colorado Springs, CO: NavPress, 2010), 143.

7. It is worth noting different translations of this verse. The Greek αγιασμός may be translated as consecration, dedication, sanctification, or holiness. The NKJV translates

"your sanctification," the NIV says "that you should be
sanctified," and the NLT renders the word "to be holy."

8. Gordon T. Smith, *The Voice of Jesus: Discernment, Prayer
   and the Witness of the Spirit* (Downers Grove, IL:
   InterVarsity Press, 2003), 76.

9. Stanford M. Lyman, *The Seven Deadly Sins: Society and
   Evil*, rev. and exp. ed. (Dix Hills, NY: General Hall,
   1989), 136.

10. Dallas Willard, *The Spirit of the Disciplines: Understanding
    How God Changes Lives* (San Francisco, CA:
    HarperSanFrancisco, 1988), 160.

11. Virginia Todd Holeman and Stephen L. Martyn,
    *Inside the Leader's Head: Unraveling Personal Obstacles to
    Ministry* (Nashville, TN: Abingdon Press, 2008), 45.

12. Simon Chan, *Spiritual Theology: A Systematic Study of the
    Christian Life* (Downers Grove, IL: InterVarsity Press,
    1998), 72.

13. Willard, *The Spirit of the Disciplines*, 191.

14. Maxie D. Dunnam and Kimberly Dunnam Reisman,
    The Workbook on the 7 Deadly Sins (Nashville, TN: Upper
    Room, 1997), 3.

15. John Cassian, *John Cassian: The Institutes*, trans. Boniface
    Ramsey (New York: Newman Press, 2000), 256.

16. Thomas Merton, *Cassian and the Fathers: Initiation
    into the Monastic Tradition*, ed. Patrick F. O'Connell
    (Kalamazoo, MI: Cistercian Publications, 2005), 156.

17. Cheslyn Jones, Geoffrey Wainwright, and Edward
    Yarnold, *The Study of Spirituality* (New York: Oxford
    University Press, 1986), 66.

Chapter 2: Pride and Humility

1. Thomas Merton, *Cassian and the Fathers: Initiation
   into the Monastic Tradition*, ed. Patrick F. O'Connell
   (Kalamazoo, MI: Cistercian Publications, 2005), 194.

2. Ibid., 196.

3. Oswald Chambers, *My Utmost for His Highest: An Updated Edition in Today's English*, ed. James Reimann (Grand Rapids, MI: Discovery House, 1992), January 12.

4. Ibid., March 8.

5. Michael W. Mangis, *Signature Sins: Taming Our Wayward Hearts* (Downers Grove, IL: InterVarsity Press, 2008), 29.

6. John Cassian, *John Cassian: The Institutes*, trans. Boniface Ramsey (New York: Newman Press, 2000), 255.

7. Ibid., 256–57.

8. Merton, *Cassian and the Fathers*, 195.

9. Steve DeNeff, *7 Saving Graces: Living Above the Deadly Sins* (Indianapolis, IN: Wesleyan Publishing House, 2010), 58.

10. Andrew Murray, *Humility* (Kensington, PA: Whitaker House, 1982), 10.

11. Charles de Foucauld, *Meditations of a Hermit* (London; Burns; New York: Orbis, 1981), 92.

12. See the first book in this set, *The Quest for Holiness—From Shallow Belief to Mature Believer*, chapter 7, "The Assurance of the Love of God."

13. Merton, *Cassian and the Fathers*, 201.

14. John Webster, *Holy Scripture: A Dogmatic Sketch* (New York: Cambridge University Press, 2003), 15.

15. Murray, *Humility*, 65.

16. Ibid., 69.

17. Benedict J. Groeschel and Kevin Perrotta, *The Journey toward God: In the Footsteps of the Great Spiritual Writers—Catholic, Protestant, and Orthodox* (Ann Arbor, MI: Charis, 2000), 90.

Chapter 3: Anger and Patience

1. Kenneth J. Collins, *Soul Care: Deliverance and Renewal through the Christian Life* (Wheaton, IL: Victor Books, 1995), 92.

2. Ibid.

3. Maxie D. Dunnam and Kimberly Dunnam Reisman, *The Workbook on the 7 Deadly Sins* (Nashville, TN: Upper Room, 1997), 77.

4. Michael W. Mangis, *Signature Sins: Taming Our Wayward Hearts* (Downers Grove, IL: InterVarsity Press, 2008), 36.

5. John Cassian, *John Cassian: The Institutes*, trans. Boniface Ramsey (New York: Newman Press, 2000), 201.

6. M. Robert Mulholland Jr., *The Deeper Journey: The Spirituality of Discovering Your True Self* (Downers Grove, IL: InterVarsity Press, 2006), 33.

7. https://www.guideposts.org/inspiration/stories-of-hope /guideposts-classics-corrie-ten-boom-on-forgiveness ?nopaging=1, accessed May 30, 2016.

8. Thomas à Kempis, *The Imitation of Christ in Four Books: A Translation from the Latin*, rev. ed., ed. Joseph N. Tylenda (New York: Vintage Books, 1998), 48.

9. Walter J. Ciszek and Daniel L. Flaherty, *He Leadeth Me: An Extraordinary Testament of Faith* (San Francisco, CA: Ignatius Press, 1995), 30.

10. Ibid., 56.

11. Ibid., 77.

12. Ibid., 116.

13. Ibid., 173.

14. Ibid., 70.

15. Andrew Murray, *Humility* (Kensington, PA: Whitaker House, 1982), 31–32.

16. Steve DeNeff, *7 Saving Graces: Living Above the Deadly Sins* (Indianapolis, IN: Wesleyan Publishing House , 2010), 23.

Chapter 4: Lust and Purity

1. Michael W. Mangis, *Signature Sins: Taming Our Wayward Hearts* (Downers Grove, IL: InterVarsity Press, 2008), 158.

2. Steve DeNeff, *7 Saving Graces: Living Above the Deadly Sins* (Indianapolis, IN: Wesleyan Publishing House, 2010), 93.

3. Maxie D. Dunnam, and Kimberly Dunnam Reisman, *The Workbook on the 7 Deadly Sins* (Nashville, TN: Upper Room, 1997), 138.

4. Dallas Willard, *The Spirit of the Disciplines: Understanding How God Changes Lives* (San Francisco, CA: HarperSanFrancisco 1988), 170.

5. Mel Lawrenz, *The Dynamics of Spiritual Formation* (Grand Rapids, MI: Baker Books, 2000), 51.

6. Oswald Chambers, *My Utmost for His Highest: An Updated Edition in Today's English*, ed. James Reimann (Grand Rapids, MI: Discovery House, 1992), September 3.

7. *The Cloud of Unknowing: With the Book of Privy Counsel*, trans. Carmen Acevedo Butcher, 1st ed. (Boston, MA: Shambhala Publications, 2009), 32.

8. Ibid., 48.

9. Richard J. Foster, *Freedom of Simplicity* (San Francisco, CA: Harper Collins, 1981), 18.

10. John R. W. Stott, *Romans: God's Good News for the World* (Leicester: InterVarsity Press, 1994), 202.

11. See *The Quest for Holiness—From Shallow Belief to Mature Believer*, chapter 6, for consideration of the means of grace and their role in the transformation of the heart.

12. Foster, *Freedom of Simplicity*, 138.

13. Dunnam and Reisman, *The Workbook on 7 Deadly Sins*, 141.

14. Chambers, *My Utmost for His Highest*, February 7.

15. Mangis, *Signature Sins*, 47.

16. See *The Quest for Holiness—From Shallow Belief to Mature Believer*, chapter 2, for further discussion of the challenge that our rational mind might bring to obedience to God.

17. George MacDonald, *The Heart of George MacDonald*, ed. Rolland Hein (Vancouver, BC: Regent College Publishing, 2004), 355.

18. Lawrenz, *The Dynamics of Spiritual Formation*, 145–46.

19. John Wesley, "On a Single Eye," Sermon 118.

20. M. Robert Mulholland Jr., *The Deeper Journey: The Spirituality of Discovering Your True Self* (Downers Grove, IL: InterVarsity Press, 2006), 106.

Chapter 5: Envy and Brotherly Love

1. M. Robert Mulholland Jr., *The Deeper Journey: The Spirituality of Discovering Your True Self* (Downers Grove, IL: InterVarsity Press, 2006), 30–42.

2. Steve DeNeff, *7 Saving Graces: Living Above the Deadly Sins* (Indianapolis, IN: Wesleyan Publishing House, 2010), 128.

3. Anselm C. Hagedorn and Jerome H. Neyrey, "'It Was Out of Envy That They Handed Jesus Over' (Mark 15.10): The Anatomy of Envy and the Gospel of Mark," *Journal for the Study of the New Testament* 69 (Mar. 1998): 17.

4. Kenneth J. Collins, *Soul Care: Deliverance and Renewal through the Christian Life* (Wheaton, IL: Victor Books, 1995), 86.

5. Ibid., 87.

6. Michael W. Mangis, *Signature Sins: Taming Our Wayward Hearts* (Downers Grove, IL: InterVarsity Press, 2008), 34.

7. Ibid.

8. Ibid., 32.

9. Ibid.

10. Maxie D. Dunnam and Kimberly Dunnam Reisman, *The Workbook on the 7 Deadly Sins* (Nashville, TN: Upper Room, 1997), 55.

11. Collins, *Soul Care*, 87.

12. Mangis, *Signature Sins*, 33.

13. Dunnam and Reisman, *The Workbook on the 7 Deadly Sins*, 53.

14. Mangis, *Signature Sins*, 155.

15. Robert A. Muthiah, *The Sabbath Experiment: Spiritual Formation for Living in a Non-Stop World* (Eugene, OR: Cascade Books, 2015), 16.

16. Collins, *Soul Care*, 88.

17. Audrey Beslow, *Change Your Bad Habits for Good!* (Nashville, TN: Abingdon Press, 1989), 149.

18. Thomas à Kempis, *The Imitation of Christ in Four Books: A Translation from the Latin*, rev. ed., ed. Joseph N. Tylenda (New York: Vintage, 1998), 89.

19. DeNeff, *7 Saving Graces*, 133.

20. Mangis, *Signature Sins*, 33.

Chapter 6: Greed and Generosity

1. Donald Capps and Melissa Haupt, "The Deadly Sins: How They Are Viewed and Experienced Today," *Pastoral Psychology* 60.6 (2011): 795.

2. Ibid., 794.

3. George O. Folarin, "Lk 12:13–21 in the Context of Human Corruption," *Asia Journal of Theology* 24.2 (2010): 312–24, 317.

4. Ibid., 320.

5. David Platt, *Radical: Taking Back Your Faith from the American Dream* (Colorado Springs, CO: Multnomah Press, 2010), 112.

6. Folarin, "Lk 12:13-21 in the Context of Human Corruption," 321.

7. Steve DeNeff, *7 Saving Graces: Living Above the Deadly Sins* (Indianapolis, IN: Wesleyan Publishing House, 2010), 71.

8. Ibid., 64.

9. Ibid., 70.

10. Gordon MacDonald and Patrick Johnson, *Generosity: Moving toward Life That Is Truly Life* (Alpharetta, GA: National Christian Foundation, 2009), 41–42.

11. Dallas Willard, *The Spirit of the Disciplines: Understanding How God Changes Lives* (San Francisco, CA: HarperSanFrancisco, 1988), 216.

12. MacDonald and Johnson, *Generosity*, 9.

13. Ibid., 11.

14. Christopher Wright, "Lausanne Theology Working Group Statement on the Prosperity Gospel," *Evangelical Review of Theology* 34.2 (2010): 99.

15. Ibid.

16. Lovemore Togarasei, "The Pentecostal Gospel of Prosperity in African Contexts of Poverty: An Appraisal," *Exchange* 40.4 (2011): 348.

17. Ibid., 99–102.

18. Jeremy Treat, "The Glory of the Cross: How God's Power Is Made Perfect in Weakness," *Christianity Today* (October 2013): 59.

19. Oswald Chambers, *My Utmost for His Highest: An Updated Edition in Today's English*, ed. James Reimann (Grand Rapids, MI: Discovery House, 1992), September 3.

Chapter 7: Gluttony and Abstinence

1. A. W. Tozer, *The Pursuit of God* (Harrisburg, PA: Christian Publications, 1982), 7.

2. Dallas Willard, "Spiritual Formation and the Warfare Between the Flesh and the Human Spirit," *Journal of Spiritual Formation and Soul Care* 6.2 (Spring 2013): 152.

3. Mel Lawrenz, *The Dynamics of Spiritual Formation* (Grand Rapids, MI: Baker Books, 2000), 51.

4. Jeff Cook, "Gluttony: It's Not Just about Eating Too Much," *Relevant* (Sept./Oct. 2009): 63.

5. John Cassian, *John Cassian: The Institutes*, trans. Boniface Ramsey (New York: Newman Press, 2000), 118.

6. Ibid., 122.

7. Ibid., 129.

8. Ibid., 120.

9. *The Cloud of Unknowing: With the Book of Privy Counsel*, trans. Carmen Acevedo Butcher, 1st ed. (Boston, MA: Shambhala Publications, 2009), 32.

10. Cook, "Gluttony," 63.

11. Michael Mangis, *Signature Sins: Taming Our Wayward Hearts* (Downers Grove, IL: InterVarsity Press, 2008), 39.

12. Maxie D. Dunnam and Kimberly Dunnam Reisman, *The Workbook on the 7 Deadly Sins* (Nashville, TN: Upper Room, 1997), 161.

13. Mangis, *Signature Sins*, 14.

14. Willard, "Spiritual Formation and the Warfare Between the Flesh and the Human Spirit," 156.

15. Ibid.

16. Ibid.

17. Richard J. Foster, *Freedom of Simplicity* (San Francisco, CA: Harper Collins, 1981), 138.

18. James Barr, "Is God a Liar? (Genesis 2–3)—and Related Matters," *Journal of Theological Studies* 57.1 (2006): 3.

19. Willard, "Spiritual Formation and the Warfare Between the Flesh and the Human Spirit," 158.

Chapter 8: Sloth and Perseverance

1. Mel Lawrenz, *The Dynamics of Spiritual Formation* (Grand Rapids, MI: Baker Books, 2000), 145–46.

2. Gordon T. Smith, *The Voice of Jesus: Discernment, Prayer, and the Witness of the Spirit* (Downers Grove, IL: InterVarsity Press, 2003), 74.

3. Augustine, *Confessions*, 50.

4. This is a North American idiom that refers to a person who spends a great amount of time watching television.

5. Quoted in Paola Azzone, "Sin of Sadness: Acedia vel Tristitia between Sociocultural Conditionings and Psychological Dynamics of Negative Emotions," *Journal of Psychology & Christianity* 31.1 (2012): 16–30, 26.

6. Quoted in Carolyn Arends, "Hardworking Sloths: How Our Busyness Can Disguise Spiritual Laziness," *Christianity Today* (June 2011): 64.

7. Michael W. Mangis, *Signature Sins: Taming Our Wayward Hearts* (Downers Grove, IL: InterVarsity Press, 2008), 52.

8. Azzone, "Sin of Sadness," 23.

9. Thomas Merton, *Cassian and the Fathers: Initiation into the Monastic Tradition*, ed. Patrick F. O'Connell (Kalamazoo, MI: Cistercian, 2005), 179.

10. Jeff Vogel, "The Speed of Sloth: Reconsidering the Sin of Acedia," *Pro Ecclesia* 18.1 (2009): 50–68.

11. Ibid.

12. Ibid., 57.

13. Ibid., 52.

14. Ibid., 65.

15. Ibid., 67.

16. Ibid.